v v v

The More I Forget, the More I Remember

v v v

Copyright 2023

This book is a work of fiction. Names, characters, places, and incidents either are products of the author's imagination or are used fictitiously. Any resemblance to actual events or locals or persons, living or dead, is entirely coincidental.

All rights reserved, including the right of reproduction in whole or in part in any form.

Foreword

Some of us are more forgetful than others.

For me, forgetting becomes a kind of mindfulness – I'm able to experience the world around me for the first time, like a child. The vivid colors of spring are brand new each year after months of only snow and dark skeletal branches reaching to the sky.

A source of wonder is important for good poetry, and even if you haven't totally forgotten something, you can choose to see life through these "eyes of a child."

Remembering can be a connection to the world around us, a shared human experience of change that brings us together. Things like school starting back up, or putting up Christmas lights - when we do these things in parallel, we connect to the shared experience of our community.

For me this is a fascinating and inspiring aspect of poetry – the voice, the explaining, of our culture.

Contents

Paula Tohline Calhoun - leaf play	1
Anna Gopen - you make me hear Vivaldi	3
Sarah Fritz - Poem for Summer	6
David I Mayerhoff - Forest of the Unseen	8
Brady Bowen - Funerary Flame	10
David E. Navarro - goings-on	12
Jordanna Miller - Waves	14
Siobhan Stromquist - epithets	16
Keith Pailthorp - Vladimir's	17
David I Mayerhoff - Settling Down	18
Jonathan Phipps - day 57//buxton, north carolina	20
Brian Peter Hodgkinson - Five Cups of Kenyan Chai	22
Bonnie Jean Lee - I sip your sunrise and taste you burnt at dusk	25
Gennaro P. Raso - A Flower Child Named Free	26
Mister Colvet - oogle	28
Nancy Jackson - An Old Woman and Her Bookshop	30
Philippe R Hebert - Summer Musing	34
Jenni Taylor - Storm Strike	36
Bonnie Jean Lee - Winnowed	38
Bonnie Jean Lee - And Juniper said to the Carpenter	40
Marta Green - Big Bear Mountain	42
Gennaro P. Raso - Laments of an ancient warrior	43
Tiger Shea Kohler - the hitchhiker	44
Miriam Kilmer - Virginia: Colors of the Seasons	46
Gennaro P. Raso - The Longest Day	49
Madelyn Paine - Forest	50
Paul Goetzinger - Snowfall on Foothills	52
Gennaro P. Raso - Annette	54
Horatio Millin - Fog & Silence	56
Beitman - the elevated wooden walkway	59

Lorri Ventura - Hermit in the Woods	60
Alwyn Barddylbach - El Rio de Luz	62
Sasha Logan - Guttersnipe	64
Margaret Davidson - It's Ducky	65
Sasha Logan - Skipping Rocks	66
David Thomas - Walking To The Border	67
Jim Beitman - The yellow silk box	69
Crystal McCollom - Apologetic October	70
Michael G. Deegan - Lilly	72
Yvette Louise Melech - In The Evening Light	73
Joelene Smith - Wolves at bay	75
Hope Soul - Mad poet	77
Marie-Jo Dorismond - Adrift	79
Alwyn Barddylbach - Flowers in the Sun	80
Rachel K. Martin - White Eyeballs	82
S. Libellule - Memories	83
Laura Sanders - Mushroom picking in the 1970's	84
Lori Ann Berti - Native Mountain	86
Jennifer Bastedo - Marvelous Picture Jasper	88
Rachel K. Martin - Always Amuses	89
Kayo Ono - Nocturne	90
Maurice Hadley - Feelings, thoughts and pains that haunt	91
AJ Calvano - Heartless	92
Bobbie Breden - Up the Winding Road	94
Nadia Washington - Down at the river	96
S. Libellule - Memorie	98
Irwin De Gannes - Out Of Mind, Into Sight	100
Lorri Ventura - (haiku)	101
April Hamlin-Sache - Love Like Rain	102
Paul Crocker - Who Took My Heart Away?	104
Marta Green - But You Said You Loved Me	106
Mia Emily - that boy who swears by his wit, wisdom, and willpower	108

Lockdown Larcs - Walking The Wait	110
Andrew lee Joyner - Life support	112
Ashley Vella - Taunting Voices	113
Angel Williams - the other father	114
Nick J. Vincelli - channeling e. e. cummings	115
Jamal Mohammed Siddiqui - Errors of Mankind	118
Lisa F. Raines - Arizona Sunset	119
Douglas R Colthurst - A Focus in Fluidity	120
Saffron E Morris - Poetic Passion	122
Michael A. Mannen - King of the snow	124
Bobbie Breden - Lost in Le Louche ~~ Free Verse	125
William E Roberts - A portrait of me	128
Sean Cooke - Autumn Leaf	130
Brian Shaun Watson - A Beautiful August Day	131
Kelsey Jean - Sunrise	132
TS Darling - Storm	133
Patricia Marie Batteate - Do You Remember	134
Rachel K. Martin - The Bee and The Hummingbird	136
Bobbie Breden - Painful in Pink ~~ Free Verse	138
Haze Le'Shay - Loving You	140
Annabelle Molyneux - US Army	141
Lorri Ventura - (haiku 2)	143
Mary L. Steffen - dinosaur dance	144
Bobbie Breden - the existential parade	145
Lisa F. Raines - Young Graduate	148
Erica Byrne - Seeing of truth	150
Paula Rowlands - Your Show	151
Dr. Michelle Wendy Hacker - In Pursuit of the Lyrical Life	152
Tor Arne Jørgensen - Footprints on broken paths	154
Stephanie Campbell - My Body Yet No Longer My Choice	155
Alessandro Chimienti - Your Caress	157
S. Libellule - Unforgotten	158
Sherin Dawn - My Crescent of Happiness	160

Nadia Washington - Silk web of the star-lit night	162
Harrison Green - Special Catch	163
S. Libellule - Memory..	165
Amathaunta Creator - Last Meltdown... Reincarnation	166
Emma Ryan - Pathological Liar	168
Madilyn Sulda - Red Roses	171
Stewart Brennan - To Wear the Mask of the Dead	173
Glenn Houston Folkes - Don't Forget	174
Sharon Diaz - Ode to 'My Loose Woman'	175
Moss M. Jacques - Our Story	176
Garnet Goode - Lost and Found	178
Matthew Broughton - Memories of You	180
Ganesh Eashwar - Requiem!	182
Philippe R Hebert - Christmas of 1958	183
Bobbie Breden - Lost in the Fire ~~ Free Verse	184
Rachel Claire - Dimentia	186
Robert Buck - time peace	188
S. Libellule - Memory	197
William Connelly, PhD - The Fledgling Finally Flies	198
Martha Enedina Gaytan - My Daughter	200
Lisa F. Raines - Will you give love and stay?	203
Rhiannon Bishop - Ghost on a cliff	204
Shanayah P. Tyrna-Denman - Have you ever heard of the crying river fairy?	206
Jeremy Geld - Hatred	208

[Paula Tohline Calhoun]

leaf play

so bold   you should - could have waited
(half-cocked careless)
scarlet. . . orange. . . purple. . . gold
too early showing your hand
patience could - would - maybe win out
(did you know the game you played)
you were not glimpsed by   loved
never feeling knowing peeping eyes
fixed adoration

rusting leaves upon the fading
grass crackle underfoot
lost in piles. . .   rain soaked. . . ignored
you must reap your value   dis-re-solve
play seasons poker once more (next chance maybe)

finish your banquet   sated
(leaving - leave - leaf   last at table)
impress upon the earth
(this is no dealer's game)
all you could be   until yet again
vermillion jack finds ace of jade
in winter's end-game

Paula T. Calhoun resides in Waynesville, NC with her husband of 47 years. She is mother to three sons, grandmother to one granddaughter. She has been writing poetry and short stories since childhood. Allpoetry.com/Paula_T._Calhoun

[Anna Gopen]

you make me hear Vivaldi

I.

chlorine mingled
with the sauce-laden air
smoke tendrils part
and I first saw you

cyan velour drapes
like the July sky
around thin body frame
as granny-smith apple eyes
crinkle above angled cheeks and
a stretching smile

laughs weave into
the periwinkle night
the story of us
begins

II.

college unfolds
on a forested campus
and in a tiny cinderblock room
our bodies curl

like twisted vines
on jersey-knit sheets

October sun streams
washing us
in the golden reflection
of new love

III.

brisk ocean spray
scents January days
driving along the coast
my hand covering
trembling fingers
like a glove

the wind whips
turquoise locks
like storming waves
and my head turns
to face you
drinking in quiet profile
letting you settle
in my veins

IV.

savoring light April rains
sprinkling down like
shooting stars

my petal lips brush
dewy mouth
curving nose
glowing brow
we blossom like
perennial flowers
finding strength
in our entwined roots

_____

Anna Gopen lives in the Bay Area, California. She has been writing poetry since the 90s. Mostly influenced by the love, sadness, and beauty in life and the world around her. Allpoetry.com/forgotten_dream

[Sarah Fritz]

Poem for Summer

I wanted to know you in the summer;
feel our fingers interlaced against the slick satin
sheets bought for this kind of night.
I wanted you to meet me, know me in my summer, open-
legged, cheeks and lips burning with sun,
wild dandelion hair clinging to winter white breasts;

See our loves play in the sprinkler,
lick shaved ice,
gallop through the grass,
wonder at birds and fireflies,
and cuddle in the night when the thunder rolls;

Drink cold beer until dark
in splintered Adirondack chairs;
staying up until the night becomes silent,
and dew wets our toes.
we would smoke
and talk
and laugh
(always laughing)
and feel so warm in that cool
night.

You kiss me with salted lips,
serpent tongue leaving its trail

down my thigh;
our scent so raw, but so familiar.
Inhale the last hint of the fire pit;
hear the cicadas incendiary hum
over muffled car alarms;
over the ceiling fan's rhythmic chugging
as it cuts the humid air, unable to keep pace;
over your hot breath on my neck
and my gasps, as you know me,
completely.

I could never get warm in your fall
and froze in your winter.
And now the daffodils are headless;
the purple princess trees nearly green again,
and you are not here.

Sarah lives in Knoxville, TN with her family. She enjoys reading poetry, coincidences, live music, palm trees, patio beers, pondering life, medicine and science, and connecting with good people. Allpoetry.com/Sarah28

[David I Mayerhoff]
Forest of the Unseen

I enter the clearing
and look all about
my eye is now focused straight ahead
at this unmapped forest

soft steps on the ground
lest I awaken the hidden life
I enter the domain
of the predatory and the fleet of foot

a growl is unleashed from a cavern
in back of old bark
now just waiting to see the outline
attached to the sound

squirrels in bunches gliding past me
like I wasn't there
some carrying chipmunks in their jaws

I walk ahead onto open land
with the sun shining bright
upon thousands of worker ants
shadowing a hill
as if waiting for orders

marching onward
I enter a cool ravine
with water rushing past
as if in a hurry
to get away from the scene

I reach the other side of the woods
panting the sigh of done
while setting my sights on the shadow
with no source for the silhouette

I quicken my pace back to the others

David I Mayerhoff is a literary writer and poet, established scientific author, and a Clinical Professor of Psychiatry. He grew up on Long Island and now resides in New Jersey.
Allpoetry.com/David_Mayerhoff

[Brady Bowen]

Funerary Flame

I lit myself afire today
to burn off all the dross
around my pyre I danced and played
and never felt the loss

The first flare of orange flower
was false pride taking flame
this thing that choked off my power
and caused me to lay blame

When next I saw my rage burn red
set fire to all around
I laughed until my anger fled
I laid that burden down

Veangefulness turned the flames to blue
as cold as winter's bite
but its grey smoke heavenward flew
like incense in the night

Next fearfulness burned yellow-bright
as it raced through my veins
true closeness won't put me to flight
or hold me with its chains

Purple raged my burning conceit
giving off acrid smells
I looked upon my inner self
and laughed like ringing bells

Green flames erupted from my eyes
a shocking sight to see
burning like bottle rockets launched
destroying crass envy

tall columns of blackest burning
I saw with my third eye
It was my cruelty exiting
a rattlesnake's long sigh

At long last the flames took their rest
departing for Hades
I realized what's left is best
and slipped ME on with ease.

_____

Brady lives in Youngsville, Louisiana. He loves to write about love, loss and living. For Colleen-you struck the first match in a slow burn. Thank you. Allpoetry.com/Brady_Bowen

[David E. Navarro]

goings-on

ee cummings and goings
on
no punctuation
this punctuality of words
under
forced punc-tu-a-tion]
seem:ing ab(surd)

come-as-you-are
early... or... late
no caps needed
no shoes no shirts no nothing

leave all the commas periods and eras
behind
for clown to p L a Y with

clown likes punctuation playthings
and wears his CAPS with pride
and ego telling others

to look
into his flower

sohecanspraythem-hahaha

with his ideologies
his gram-
marred theologies
to fool them
and laugh flaff flaff
at them

come-as-you-are
raw
words
in a bag

organic MAGNANIMITY

minus caps and
hats punctuality
ee

cummings and goings
on/

David E. Navarro is a poet-philosopher, author, essayist and editor in Tucson AZ. Google/search 'David E. Navarro poet' online for a full bio and links to his books and work. Allpoetry.com/D.E._Navarro

[Jordanna Miller]

Waves

The smell of saltwater fills the air, as
the waves gently brush up against his feet.
He looks out at the horizon,
and feels the grittiness of the sand
as he crumbles bits of it between his fingers.
The sound of gulls in the distance.
Their husky cries,
reverberate off the shoreline.
Into the clouds.

She watches him, watches the late afternoon sun as it highlights
his greying hair. And she's tempted to walk over.
Tempted to sit down beside him,
place her hand over his.
But then she looks out at the ocean,
and she thinks about how
many often meet their end
because they're tempted by the waves.

She doesn't go to him, but she continues to look at him.
Viewing him the way you sometimes view a body of water.
Carefully, from a distance.
Only going closer if you're certain you'll make it back out.
She's not sure she will.

And while she's admires him,
he admires the waves.
And they're both admiring unpredictable things of beauty.

Jordanna is from Townsville, Queensland. I've been writing for almost 5 years and still don't really know what I'm doing. But it makes living with myself a bit easier. Allpoetry.com/Jordanna

[Siobhan Stromquist]

epithets

the corn-mother wraps her hand around the handle
she rakes her fingers through the humus and she
rips peas from the vines.

demeter; the spender of gifts, the bearer of fruit,
a rot wipes out the harvest and the people starve.
demeter the angry.

the corn-mother withers in winter,
entombs herself in the mud and
waits to thaw.

demeter the blooming,
unfolds with the budding leaves
catches springtime in her arms.

———————————

Siobhan is a teacher from Alberta, Canada. She enjoys math, science, insects, and sometimes she writes a poem or two. Allpoetry.com/Sian_Stromkvist

[Keith Pailthorp]

Vladimir's

ascendant
who lately mounted
his chameleon camoflag-drab
tank
and decapitated onetwothreefourfive childrenjustlikethat

Rasputin
he wasn't freakishly short
and what i want to know is
how do you like your blue-eyed boy
Mister Stalin

Keith Pailthorp is a retired state bureaucrat who hangs on the banks of a man-made pond in Davis, CA. Allpoetry.com/Keith_Pailthorp

[David I Mayerhoff]
Settling Down

the green is blooming
with the cold
swept out the revolving door of nature
a swift kick in the pants
good riddance

I walk out the front door
take a deep breath in
soak up the warm breeze and rustle of leaves
as if the elements were cheering me on

it is important to have people rooting for you
or at least the trees and grass

all seen through the lens of optimism
shopping will go smooth
a nice walk amongst the new smells of spring

the sour neighbor
now waves hello like Mr. Rogers
our tiff of long ago forgotten

birds chirp the song of greeting
offer pointers on the scenery
like a museum guide
no headphone necessary

transitions seem to settle the pulse
not letting complacency
take this all for granted

David I Mayerhoff is a poet and literary writer, established scientific author and a Clinical Professor of Psychiatry. He grew up on Long Island and now resides in New Jersey. Allpoetry.com/David_Mayerhoff

[Jonathan Phipps]
day 57//buxton, north carolina

dark grey skies
rain softly falling on cape hatteras
stringman sings through walkman earbuds
drops pitter-pattering on my jacket
writing letters never sent
weather radio blares a warning
gales are coming in
lightning bolts strike the water
thunder claps rattle the bones
bumper crop of sea glass in the afterward
sitting, writing poems in the stairway of the lighthouse
as storms rage, whitecaps on the ocean

the drip of a leak echoes
through the lighted spire
wristwatch chimes seven as evening falls
maroon ships on the water
bobbing like bath toys
sharpening my pencil
with a pocket knife
three pages begats four
as the monsoon lessens
peek my head out the door
foggy ocean scenes
against a cotton-candy pink sunset
sunlight rays dying on the water

twilight sheds its skin, molting into dusk
beach chairs, umbrellas tossed
in the waterspout's wake

plastic bags, right-coast tumbleweeds
cartwheel over the dunes, past highway 12
buggies motor over the hills
hotel balcony crowds cheer
seaside drag racing
as cherry-red sprites light the horizon
over cloud tops eight miles high
bonfires down the shore
smell of burgers, cuban sandwiches
picking ukulele on my porch
connected to three rooms in buxton
waxing gibbous burns yellow
watching the tide slowly leave my backyard
pick a piece for peace

Writer, musician, poet, aspiring world changer, loving life and living love. I have made a life of using 20 words when I only needed 5, and am sincerely grateful! Allpoetry.com/tennesseefluxedo

[Brian Peter Hodgkinson]

Five Cups of Kenyan Chai

Here the snows drift higher–
watching the vortex from the north
collect inches upon feet
The dread white grows relentlessly
demands my hand-blistering shovel, but
in the floating-flake sky, I fly–

1. back in Kenya
sitting peacefully by
a lush passion fruit vine
picking the purple ornament fruits
for a tart morning smoothie

the feathered blue Turaco
croaks proudly
in the woven
dewy morning emerald leaves

the front yard the banana stalk bends
from a giant bloated purple flower,
ripening on the ground.
seeing myself breathe the African dust
my rosy sun-scalded skin,
Swahili salutations, with "Jambo!"
the "how are yous?"
family handshakes, morning grins

acceptance, hospitality, generosity
love.

the Kakamega forest nearby
of purer earth, bluer bird-filled sky –
Colobus monkeys eye down from the trees
curious heads tilt, just watch
chattering shouts one to another
a network of moss climbs up the roots of the
ancient banyan elder

I trudge through the velvet gumbo mud
& sink in,
fiery "siafu" ants run up my pants,
off with my pants - ow ow ow
they're drawing blood, but
this cowboy just grins to self
it's still better than a blizzard.

4. I'm again walking that
sour-smelling tobacco-like Mumias road,
sugarcane rustles under the cotton blue.
Marching kilometers beside
friends, so many friends,
we sit in a circle in grass-thatched huts
drinking hot chai, sweet milk tea
until foreheads bead "jasho"
sweat, grinning content,
dipping and chewing bakery road bread

we all laugh till our bellies hurt.
the fellowship flows.

pulled back to Ohio,
the shock. The muffled sounds
of scraping plows
calls me kicking here now.
The blustery snow shrieks
& armies of flakes swirl
the freeze is killing me frozen
But once upon my sunny days, I was

5. Carried away by the afternoon
dust devils of Western Kenya,
fresh, crisp air filling lungs
born of the scented black virgin soil,
which warms fertile
this snow man's
dreams.

───────────────

I'm a father of four with seven grandchildren. I lived overseas in Africa and India for over twenty years. I was involved in development work. I love to write and have a graphic imagination. Allpoetry.com/Brian_Peter_Hodgkinson

[Bonnie Jean Lee]

I sip your sunrise and taste you burnt at

dusk

You are a morning-side New England chorist
made of Willard maple pines and paper birch,
the echo of steam train whistles in forest.

Upon mountain ranges where lilac finch perch
you bloom in Hampshire roses and snowy pearls,
laced in all granite seasons 'pon which I search.

A scent that lingers in cinnamon stick swirls
as does mist to salt on burnt sienna rust,
thereupon raspberry wilts of red-wood curls.

Alas, memory and grief do what they must,
as I sip sunrise and taste you burnt at dusk.

Bonnie-Jean Lee is a Poet from New Hampshire. She enjoys all forms of literature and artistic expression. Her other passions include, Shutter Button Poetry. Allpoetry.com/Skye_Darkholme

[Gennaro P. Raso]

A Flower Child Named Free

Cherry red relaxed lips
large blue tinted sunglasses reflect the chanting crowd.
sandy brown, herbal scented hair hangs and flows,
paisley bandana decks her head.

cuff bracelets, stringed grey faux pearls, and leather twine—
stack and slide on slender forearms
thin fingers adorned with silver and turquoise rings
muffle her ears.

a white cotton halter top shields soft skin
hand woven brown leather belt hangs below her belly button—
tight faded bell bottom blue jeans
worn from sitting on grass that stained them green,
flower drops and peace sign patches on both knees

tanned animal hide Jesus sandals made in India,
display ruby painted toenails on unevenly tanned feet
silver toe rings stained by nineteen-seventies dust.

the robin egg blue transistor radio sitting
in my pocket, is Japanese made
set to 1420 rock, the booming anthems the radio played
police sirens blare reaching the protest fade
her fist in the air, she joins the hip crowd's parade.

Gennaro P. Raso started writing poetry recently to fill his time. He finds it emotionally cathartic.
Allpoetry.com/Gennaro_P_Raso

[Mister Colvet]

oogle

clarifying shampoo
cannot remove the guilt
sticking to my rough skin
and no form of soap
can wash the dried bloodpools
on my grimy stretched banjo drum
or my tattered fabric dressings
covering all the infected bug bites
and cratered red rashes growing
or the necrotic purple pits swirling
on my stretchy coat of skin
as I stare down the toilet bowl
puking up booze and bile
in a gas station bathroom
so forget deodorant
or aluminum antiperspirant
I'd rather reek forever
in the dusky carnal shrouds
tethered to the sky like a balloon animal
and look away from the commonplace
common commoner citizens
that can't bear to push past
the plastic bags stuck
to my beached whale of a soul

where the waters sting sharper
than a school of ripe jellyfish

A plain-clothes engineer, writer, artist, and general over-thinker wrapped into one epithelial sheet deemed human.

Check out my work at lastpagesofhumanity.blogspot.com! Allpoetry.com/Colvet

[Nancy Jackson]

An Old Woman and Her Bookshop

returning from my bookshop
settling down into the easy chair
 doilies on the arms need washing
when were they crocheted?
overstuffed with a prominent firm back
including arms twice the normal size
shapeless from years of me lying flat
stretched across the seat lengthwise
   it was a feat long ago
that I could easily do
but now that I've grown old
it's a flexibility I outgrew
leastwise I can still plod
to my bookshop and back
down the road near my house
   though I wish these shoes
would give me less flack
"Pages in Time" is weathered inside and out
its old yellowed chandelier
hangs precariously loose
grand in its day once now it can barely produce
enough light to read the
spines of the books on the racks

creaky planked floors lead the way
through corridors of stacks

crammed with tales of heroic lore
read by dukes and captains of the sea
doctors and motormen and brides-to-be
young boys and girls and in-betweens
   and sixty-odd years of wondrous books
which have certainly entertained me
aisles in some places so narrow they require
walking through sideways as if on a wire
pressing your back against the stack behind
to locate titles below the sightline
   once I knocked over quite a few books
onto the dusty marked floor
after crooking my neck in an attempt to see
titles of the marvelous Dame Christie
there's no place to sit and read awhile
no place to drink cafe au lait
but there is an old small metal rack half-filled
with magazines from back-in-the-day
   I picked one up once
so old and dry were the pages
they crumbled into pieces and
scattered throughout the place
first time I ventured into this mysterious store
this eight-year-old was mesmerized
   nothing has changed in sixty years
except for the dust that is deeper and
the chandelier that is dimmer
- or could it be that my eyes are just older?
an older man shuffled over to me and
said with a glint in his eye

haven't seen him for many years
he must be dead by now
"may I interest you in an adventure?"
from that moment on this
store and those books had a certain hold on me
yes, from that moment on
this store and those books
had a firm hold on me

every week since, I have returned to choose
a new book to inspect on my own
more a library than a real bookshop
each book - one at a time - is free and on loan
  never have I've seen anyone
other than myself
except of course the shopkeeper
often changing
but always old
how can they keep this shop alive
despite only one older man
no customers, no cash, not even a register
just one man and one woman - me
  how can he manage such a large place
it is a strange little store in many ways
yet even after such a long time
it still has a hold on me
this shop and those books have quite a grip
yes, they have quite a firm hold on me and

I must go back in a week, yes
I must go back in a week.

Nancy Jackson grew up by the ocean but now lives in a valley near the Smokey Mountains. Nature and life experiences frame her poetry and give voice to her spiritual life and healing journey. Allpoetry.com/Nancy_daisygirl

[Philippe R Hebert]
Summer Musing

Silver Lake
An old cottage with outbuildings
Backed up to woods of birch and aspen
An acre of grass fronts it
Encircled by split rail

Silver Lake camp
Cedar shake and
A porch screened
Hammocks within
Wood burning stove and water pump
Old Town Lapstrake runabout
Moored nearby

Early morning fog and
Dew covered all
Loons plaintive calls

A country dinner is done
This morning's fish catch
With pleasant lingering smells
The evening and night time chill
Driven off with a potbellied stove

Only the radio
Playing country tunes

With familiar conversations
An old deck of cards
And whiffs of cigars smoke

Apparent quiet
Comfort and contentment
Deceiving
The truth is tension and stress
Suppressed

The good doctor
Is stoned yet again.

Philippe R. Hebert has written over 50 technical articles that have been published in various technical magazines. He is final negotiations with a publicist for his poetry book "Homage, An Anthology". Allpoetry.com/PRHebert

[Jenni Taylor]

Storm Strike

A storm performs a ballet beyond the plain,
swirling throughout the atmosphere.

Cloud to ground lightning performs,
with tendrils groping the landscape.

Thunder rumbles in the distance,
spitting heavy rain across the sky.

The earthly smell of petrichor raindrops,
kiss the arid land in which it falls.

Ghostly ribbons of magnetic fields,
passing electricity through clouds.

Wind rushes crosswise, splitting grass,
dancing across distant meadows.

Swift changes within the warm air,
as downdraft cuts off the updraft.

Weakening outflow slowly dissipating,
rainfall decelerates into a pitter patter.

Brilliant beams of light peak beyond,
where once a storm was surging above.

Due to a car accident in 2002, I am paralyzed from the neck down. Most of my poems are about me, my accident, hope, gratitude, for contests, and life in general. Allpoetry.com/Jtay

[Bonnie Jean Lee]
Winnowed

Thereby I go, winnowed -
under the tabebuia tree,
pink salted trumpets,
unfurled in winter wreaths.

I pay, but a farthing's smile
to the strides of light -

that stitch the ridges
of ladder-back stalks,
that bow haggardly,
diminishing their height.

A nail varnish scintillation,
gaudy as it is demure -

shrilly whistling between
those hunchback Himalayas -
standing guard beyond the moor.

They peer, rueful and wry,
wrenching all the while -
a wind drummed up
to catch the eye.

And thereby I go, winnowed -
with their piercing,

yet inadvertent gaze,

stumbling to reach those crags,
perpetually elusive in its haze.

Bonnie-Jean Lee is a Poet from New Hampshire. She enjoys all forms of literature and artistic expression. Her other passions include, Shutter Button Poetry. Allpoetry.com/Skye_Darkholme

[Bonnie Jean Lee]

And Juniper said to the Carpenter

You've carved erasable bruises
against the bark of wood,

hushed seasons of winter greens
and sprouting wildflowers.

Like the death of scattered leaves
over water hemlock,

sawdust fell
beneath the cracked flooring
of toxic moments -

became displaced against itself
as if it were made of wax foundations -

as if all the while
beneath trembling,
ashen sirens,

you held the flame.

The earth now stays unsteady,
shuddering in the balefire

of your outline,

within barricades of collective grief -
insecurities left stuttering

in a shadow-diary
of unrhythmic ticks.

They resound on glass windows,
the ones you painted untouchable.

And as the marbled wainscoting
of ash and bleach double stitch -

like soot on lanterns,
it blackens the pale skin
of tracing paper -

I am left ever to wither.

Bonnie-Jean Lee is a Poet from New Hampshire. She enjoys all forms of literature and artistic expression. Her other passions include, Shutter Button Poetry. Allpoetry.com/Skye_Darkholme

[Marta Green]
Big Bear Mountain

walking on the usual path
hulking, steep, over grown forest
rushing winds sway green pine trees
off the beaten path
taking a detour to splashing falls

across the gorge
in the middle of the stone wall set back from the sheer front
formed across a millennium of environment and time
climbing down the bumpy lane
using climbing gear on the sheer wall of rock
sweating, exertion and a slip of a foot
safety harness catches a person

making it to the perfect shaped heart pond
sitting on the edge, feet in the cool wetness
like marble, smooth and polished
a little pond, thigh deep clear blue clean water

———————————

Marta Green is from the state of Texas, about an hour from the gulf coast. She loves writing poetry and short stories. Her husband and family are some of her greatest supporters! Allpoetry.com/Marta_Green

[Gennaro P. Raso]

Laments of an ancient warrior

Fight! loudly laughing my king once decreed
sixteen years young I quickly followed
grunt scream bleed
clash my sword now red against the foe.

moaning groaning lumps of men lay
silenced by the thrust of the victor's spear
my king's gaping mouth is silent, his head on a pike
vultures settle to pluck out the eyes of the dead
I grimace from the stench of burnt corpses.

no longer a warrior now a slave
bowed over I stand like wilted wheat.
watery eyes cut a path down my bloodied face,
cracked bloody hands hold heavy rusted chains

work! screams the captain flaying his cutting whip,
obey or nailed to the wood,
left like a raisin on the vine to hang, shrivel and dry.
The first and last battle for this farmer warrior slave
the only flight from the enemy's tight clutch is death.

Gennaro P. Raso started writing poetry recently to fill his time.
He finds it emotionally cathartic.
Allpoetry.com/Gennaro_P_Raso

[Tiger Shea Kohler]

the hitchhiker

driving along,
in my cherry red bug
seeing ahead on the side of the road
a man waving his thumb in the air

slowing,
easily seen were khaki pants and violet shirt
next his ivory skin and licorice hair

stopping,
he leaned down and looked at me
through the open window
shocked to see a girl
those emerald eyes were shimmering
my breath caught in my chest
he was going my way, north,
heading to Cleveland
get in I said

taking off,
on our wild, spectacular ride
how can years fly?
8 crazy ones have
still on the road we go

———————

I live in a small town in Northwest Georgia. I write for both emotional healing and just having fun. Some poems are about others and some are just my imagination but most are my truth. Allpoetry.com/Tiger_Shea

[Miriam Kilmer]

Virginia: Colors of the Seasons

When I was three, one snowfall
came as high as my waist;
the whole universe was white.
I shivered more with excitement
than with cold.
Indoors, I sought the dark brown comfort of cocoa—
the warmth of brightly-colored afghans.
No other winter has come close.

My senior year,
everything blossomed at once.
Ignoring the usual ordered progression,
daffodils and jonquils broke across the lawn,
yellow and white like the dawn,
while cherry trees wafted pale petals
on the new green grass all around.
Great billowing clumps of azaleas
in yellow, orange, pink, white,
purple, or fuchsia
popped blazing color onto nearly every lawn.
Judas trees broke forth in tiny red-violet buds,
but maples were still budding rust.
I wrote a poem about it
for my classmate's birthday.
Only a few other Springs have dazzled me as that one did.

Summer brings to mind my growing years—
children in bare feet, dungarees, and calico shirts.
Sometimes we grew a vegetable garden out back.
I can just see those bright-red strawberries
nestled, hidden among their own soft leaves.
There were rows of pale green lettuce heads
poking out of the dark earth,
fertilized and hoed.
Overhead, the English walnuts
pushed out clusters of nuts
covered with moss-green husks.
Those heavy missiles hid among their lacy fronds
waiting to bomb us.

The mountains sing to me of autumn;
leaves glow just as brightly
in the Piedmont where we live,
but mountains and valleys spread
the glory of the season
for miles around.
Evening, distance, and cloud shadows
turn the green and gold to blue.
Storms scudding overhead
paint wildly shifting patterns on the slopes.
Gashes of brilliant yellow-gold
and gilded red
stripe the shadows,
punctuated by dark evergreens.
Rain pelts down in sheets, almost opaque,

burnishing the leaves like ancient treasure.
Atop the Blue Ridge, we prowled the parking lot
seeking out stags
with ivory antlers tiered like chandeliers.
We trod through piles of fallen leaves,
yellow and brown on the withering grass.

Now it is Autumn in the Piedmont,
between the mountains and the shore.
Outside our window, we catch glimpses
of the season's syncopated morphing
from splendor to muted hues.
With conflicted feelings,
we anticipate
the cold fingers of winter
with its wind-bent icicles
and softly drifting snow.

Miriam Kilmer grew up in Northern VA in a large family steeped in the arts. Her ancestors include poets Joyce Kilmer and Aline Kilmer. She lives with husband Tim Slattery and their two rescue cats. Allpoetry.com/Miriam_Kilmer

[Gennaro P. Raso]

The Longest Day

White centered orange star glows—
rises slowly at dusk smiles bright,
warms my droopy face mists eyes blurs sight—
cheeks pull apart,
gaping mouth elongated shaped like a slice of tangerine.

Clouds like school children at breaktime—
play peek-a-boo with the burly sturdy golden flare in the blue,
shadow and light laughs, taunts below glides back and forth.
Earth's top tilts toward the sky king this June day
the longest the orb is out to play.

Sunshine like spears let fly fire down,
eyes snap shut, inner eyelids mingle pools of citrus hues.
Noon sun seated stout is king of the mountain sky—
my body's dark trail like a sundial's shadow swings,
from short to tall and back to short.

Darkness creeps, shy sol descends deep, hides behind night—
sky turns blue to black the close of longest day in sight.
Full bloom of moon blemished
by floating gray streaks of dust and dead lead haze—
signals the arrival of solstice's end and shorter days.

―――――――――――

Gennaro P. Raso started writing poetry recently to fill his time.
He finds it emotionally cathartic.
Allpoetry.com/Gennaro_P_Raso

[Madelyn Paine]

Forest

The calmness of the green
The sap oozes down the outer bark
The roots of the old trees
Cold water rushes down in the abandoned creek

Sticks and stones scratch my ankles
Ticks climb into my skin
Raccoons rummage through the leaves

Birds chirp in the thick canopy
Broken logs crash down in the swamp
Twigs snapping under my feet

The trees stand tall
Bugs swarm my head
Dipping in and out of my view

Dirt smudging on my hands
Fish swim in the creek
Rabbits hop around with their furry little paws

The sunshine through the canopy
The snake's skin glistens in the sun
A small breeze swooshes my hair

Astray wires cut my hands
Old wood frames trip my feet
Tires taking up space in the field

Broken metal fences lean against the old oak tree
Where they came from nobody knows
Just another mystery
Of the forest

Toads and frogs croak aloud
Muddy water splashes up my leg
Dripping down in my shoes, soaking my socks

At night time the forest glistens in the moonlight
Water sits still as a feather
All sounds are muted
All the animals sleep in their little homes
That's the forest

I'm a middle school student from Canton, Michigan. I find great happiness in poetry. I love expressing my interests and feelings through my poems to share with others. Allpoetry.com/Poet369

[Paul Goetzinger]
Snowfall on Foothills

Blustery winter storm invades
Painting a sprinkling of snow
On lowlands
Stranding motorists on icy highways
Schools close
Foothills freeze under icy blankets

Bundled up children
Explode out of houses
Cheeks rosy from the cold
Making forts
For snowball fights
Making snowmen
For ornaments
Sledding on Himalayan sized hills

Sons and daughters
Scaling snowy slopes
In morning hours
On unplowed roads
Tree limbs falling
From weight of fallen snow
Arctic winds
Drop temperatures
While citizens snap selfie photos of snow-covered lawns

Paul Goetzinger is a freelance writer and educator from Des Moines, Washington. He has written articles for magazines and other publications for the past 18 years. Allpoetry.com/Paul_Goetzinger

[Gennaro P. Raso]

Annette

The gold topaz bracelet she wore calls to me,
the fragrance of flowery perfume
slowly surfaces like her soft smile.

the bouquet unseals the vault of my memory
the day the tiny red bottle's mist caressed her wrist
kissed her slender, soft neck
imbuing the air as she walked through it

alive like a droopy plant watered
the scent brings forth the vision of Annette

muddy rusted spade in hand,
grandmother's large straw hat
on her yellow carnation hair—
like her garden of blooms, wavy and vibrant.

adorning a flower-patterned sun dress
blending in the colors—
pink, purple, yellow white orange
blossoms, like little children surround her.

Stephanotis genus multiplied in her garden
the botanical nomenclature
flowed from her tongue like a violin solo.

I smile and wipe my wet eyes and face
put the bracelet and bottle in place.

looking out of the bedroom window,
a white crown shaped flower sprouts as hundreds once stood
it reaches toward the sun smiling.

Gennaro P. Raso started writing poetry recently to fill his time.
He finds it emotionally cathartic.
Allpoetry.com/Gennaro_P_Raso

[Horatio Millin]
Fog & Silence

from: 'History of a Christian Rebel'

Dew drips.
Drops big enough
for sensing by skin.
Tiny ant-ninjas on patrol.
Below resolutions of sight.

Fog conspires
w/ trees in the bayou:
contrast decreases,
color wanes to ashen green.
Slugs emboldened to appear
from their invertebrate dimension
under cover of intemperate moistures.

Moving slowly,
with the solitary grace of a monk.

Other-worldly.
Time & color appears connected:
color dims,
seconds expand to lethargy.

Trees branches ominously still
wind slowed to a creeping gasp:

time slowed its motion
molecules dance upon the ether.
Air shudders in place:
trapped within a deep torpor.

Silence is over-large.
Sucking decibels
into its cavernous maw.
Vertiginous silence sucking sound
to inevitable expulsion
on the other side of the world.

Coppery decibels
receive their crush
in machineries of silence
without roar,
or question.

The sap in trees can be heard,
resonant,
like marrow in the bones,
moving their microscopic mysteries:
turbulent thumping:
proteins on a membrane
trampoline.
Mitotic snapping of cells:
ionic crackle
of mitochondrial energies
in follicles of noisy jitter.

Blood & sap
operate outside
the law
& deaf ears
of fog & silence.
⊙

Horatio Millin is from St. Thomas, USVI. Poetry helps me record the landscapes of the heart. I enjoy calligraphy as alternate art form. Allpoetry.com/talysman

[Jim Beitman]
the elevated wooden walkway

the elevated wooden walkway
meanders through the dense
tropical forest gently brushing
by the giant ferns orchids
and coconut palms all smiling
their waxy leaves toward the sun
while bending gracefully around
the thick plants on the jungle base
that make up the soft green carpet
that ties together the living floor

I am an artist living in Noblesville Indiana. Writing is a great media that helps distill my feelings, thoughts, and experiences. It is always a great thrill to be included in an Allpoetry anthology! Allpoetry.com/Beitmanjim

[Lorri Ventura]
Hermit in the Woods

Despite the rumor that she ate children
I looked for her
As I rode my horse along the overgrown, old, lumberjack trail.
Once I saw her drifting toward me among the towering oaks
At first I thought she was a rag-clad ghost
Her skin translucent
Waist-length hair colorless
And adorned with brown leaves.
Nostrils flared,
My palomino shied away from her fusty odor.
As if possessed,
I slowly reached into my saddle bag.
Hands trembling,
I held out the carrot packed
As a treat for my mount.
The woman crept toward me
Then, fast as a beam of light,
She grabbed with a vine-like hand,
And devoured the root tuber.
Subtly tugging on the bridle's reins,
I backed up,
Worried that the specter was eyeing me
As her lunch entree.
But then she dropped to her knees,
Head bowed and hands clasped as if in prayer

Giving me both leave and benediction.
I never told my parents,
Knowing that they'd forbid me ever again to ride in the forest
But whenever I rode down that path
I packed an extra sandwich or snack
In case the woman re-appeared.
Never again did she grace me with her presence
No matter how hard I searched.

―――――――――

Lorri Ventura is a retired special education administrator living in Massachusetts. Her writing has been featured in a number of publications. She has won three Moon Prizes for her poetry. Allpoetry.com/Lorri_Ventura

[Alwyn Barddylbach]
El Rio de Luz

Let's sit on a snow cloud crescent moon
so we can see the sun bake in the west,
crimson cassock around burning burrow of flames.
From the east bridal dawn chases the Titan torch,
river of light, great glittering arch of Milky Way over Cotopaxi
for aching love of Io -

I see you.

My seat is a refuge on the ice summit
of a scorching quaking Andean mountain.
My molten belly sinks into the gaping breadth
and crevice of Rio Negro steamy Amazon forest,
under sweltering bark and shade,
ancestral spirit of the great kapok tree -

And there I see you.

Let's catch the first and last light
of this blue planet from the watchful rim
of a poet's eye, fly by Galileo -

Skim raindrops of Methuselan sweat
together, spin around
and dive off sparkling vertigo rivers
into salty warm drifts and depths of naked ocean.

The passage of life to die for,
on the edge is fragrant, wild and free -

I see you still.

Skip off a smouldering frosty volcano ring of fire,
forging a vision from dark rock on solar flares
in the rift of the valley between you and I.

Stretch out the canvas and there I will be -

riding on the promise
of tomorrow.

———————

Cotopaxi is one of the highest active stratovolcanoes on earth - sender of fire and rain, a place where gods lived and a new year dawns, AB. Allpoetry.com/Barddylbach

[Sasha Logan]

Guttersnipe

guttersnipe
toothpick
pocket knife

punk rock
plaid socks
hip hop

mice of men
on again
off again

mosh pit
limp wrist
fell on it

studs and spikes
motorbike
guttersnipe

Pansexual nomad. Writing random thoughts. No rhyme or reason. Rent in America is sucks. Crime in America is outrageous. Bigots are awful. Peace to all. amazon.com/author/SashaLogan Allpoetry.com/Sasha_Logan

[Margaret Davidson]

It's Ducky

Three wild types of duck: mallard, tern, and merganser
Adam Cartwright was my first crush on TV's Bonanza
Any bird one calls a drake is a mature male duck
Want more of my cash? Here you're out of luck
One hominid reproductive action is a quick _uck
The yellow glue has dried : All the boards are stuck
The number of prongs on one antler age one deer, a buck
All the white Leghorn hens are dead, no emitted cluck
Chicken Of The Sea tuna has no feathers to pluck
All the stable stalls are used. All ready! Time to muck
For needed prayer Robin Hood used one Friar Tuck
To slowly lick a lollypop is to savor that suck
The bull rider was unseated by the crossbreed's final buck
Scarlet red is the color of a firefighter's laddered truck
Ears of corn and shell clams are harvested. Time to shuck
No visible open net ice hockey shot. Pass the puck
One of Austria's cities is the burg Innsbruck
The Axis leader Adolf Hitler was a totalitarian schmuck
I'm sick to death of all this stinking garbage. Where's a truck
Muddle through that final puddle! JUMP don't DUCK

I'm a 75 year old widow who enjoys the written word. Poetry is my catharsis. Ducks have a shorter neck than geese. .Read ' The Ugly Duckling'. Allpoetry.com/Margaret_M_Davidson

[Sasha Logan]

Skipping Rocks

skipping rocks
skips cut
ripples in the loch.

find the flats
a flick of my wrist
send them speeding past.

over logs
and lily pads
don't knock the frog.

from the beach
cast the pebble
past the sprouting reeds.

skipping stones
to pass the day
wouldn't change a thing.

―――――――――

5 squads left and the ring is looking small. Rent in America is high. Crime in America is high. Write every day.

Amazon.com/author/SashaLogan
Allpoetry.com/Sasha_Logan

[David Thomas]
Walking To The Border

We are students of the order
uninsured, standing in line
border beings marching forward
taxed and vaxxed
sneakered and freed
looking for tranquility.

Pols don't see us moving by
invisible to camera's eye.
Ghostly winged post citizen
already injected death within.

Still we march toward the goal
newborn wraiths silently stroll.
Up and down through walls and hills
unrecorded holes to fill.

Suddenly in the vineyard isle
where never are we seen at all.
Moving past dark hills and plains
arising from the fields of grain.

Not seen flying out of view
mothers children laughing too.
Leaving gated homes behind
finding safety in the sky.

David grew up in a small New England town in the 1950's and moved to Virginia soon afterwards. He worked at a VA Med Center for many years and is now retired. He enjoys writing in the countryside.   Allpoetry.com/Davidlind

[Jim Beitman]

The yellow silk box

The yellow silk box
Wrapped in tangerine ribbon
Happily joined the little girls
On tiny chairs
To join the party
With its contents organized
In satin sleeves
Three generations old
Contained the dainty porcelain
Cups and saucers
Held with pinkies high
They Laughed and giggled
The same elegant excitement
And gracious manners
That all the women
In the family practiced
At that special age
With that special
Silk ribboned box

———————

I am an artist living in Noblesville Indiana. Writing is a great media that helps distill my feelings, thoughts, and experiences. It is always a great thrill to be included in an Allpoetry anthology! Allpoetry.com/Beitmanjim

[Crystal McCollom]
Apologetic October

feeble light struggles with moody grey clouds
as forces of change are in the air
creating the sounds of the season
speaking in low forceful tones

spider webs catch buds, but summer will not stay
a genocide of nature
holds dominion over the land
soil settles to sleep

October wavers between duty and regret
between gusts of emotion and
dangling kisses of wonder
reluctant

one last rose
one last dahlia
glittering with their dusting
of glistening flakes of snow

arbitrator of the season
the tamaracks
burst into golden splendour
snaring October's storm eye
signalling the time to move on

order and life can only be balanced
by chaos and death
the energy of beauty
has gone to ground

I write poetry or need to write poetry when I am emotionally aroused or sweating droplets of curiosity. I paint when there are no words left to express what is inside. Ontario Canada
Allpoetry.com/Nannanorse

[Michael G. Deegan]

Lilly

on a crisp fall day
wind whipping around the bare branches
gray clouds hang above
sun rays alive between the cracks
Lilly singing a tune in the kitchen
she is lonely as a falling soldier
so many tears she cries
Lilly makes way to the cellar
in the dim light she sits on a short stool
in the corner a spider's web
she can hear the rain fall on the sill
the damp air lofts above
the thick hand-hewn rafter above
the rope hangs tight
the wooden stool lays silent on its side
the rain still falls the clouds black
Lillys body hangs with no life

On a crisp fall day
I think of Lilly often

I am from New England, I enjoy writing poems and short stories.
I have a collection from the 1970's to the present.
This is my first attempt at making them available for all to enjoy.
Allpoetry.com/REDdog_425

[Yvette Louise Melech]

In The Evening Light

I'm sitting on a dark wooden chair was once a weapon for hypnotising customers in exotic artistic tanks

A tightly dressed apron thrilled white frilly black short skirt high heeled female fatale.

Make those heels black said her boss.

Patent will act as one's tool to seduce
artistically inclined minds hanging out of coffee cups drooling over my arty pieces.

T'was an art cafe in heyday moments hanging
In dreamland.

Two thousand and twelve I sucked myself under tables with legs that twisted round and around.
Those waitresses with small hips,
as mine are now, wore thickened brimmed spy glasses.

In the evening light sitting over London Bridge.
One reminces on many a pound buster.
That was dragged to the floor.
Jealous scoundrels
till the cake bakes.
London lights.

City nights.
One wonders where I will be tomorrow.

We're not leaving in the moonlight now.

Yvette Louise Melech is from London UK. Having Scottish and Polish Parents. She holds a devoted interest in the Art world. Brought up in the world of art from both parents' work and interests. Allpoetry.com/Doll_In_The_Cupboard

[Joelene Smith]

Wolves at bay

the world is covered in frozen sheets of hell
snow blinds the eyes of the terrified man
wolves howl and race for flesh

Snarling
Gnash
Screams

blood drips and turns the snow red

Snarling
Gnash
Screams

sheets of the frozen hell engulfing

Terrified
Starved
Bleeding

unforgiving snow blinds

the water beneath beckons
yet unable to claim,
black and white wolves encompass like a ying-yang
nowhere to hide,
starving to death

―――――――――――

Joelene Smith is from Cody, Wyoming. She has six kids and a cat. She loves the outdoors and prefers writing then people. Allpoetry.com/Joelene_Smith

[Hope Soul]
Mad poet

he calls himself a lunatic
with eyes drunk off warm sangria
whatever the trick
just make it stick
even if it makes him sick
gulp it down
drip
drop
channels of red
running down your chin
gladly challenging the night sky
howls at the arguing moon

click goes the fire stick
giggles till it hurts
plum red cheeks
matching blood shot eyes
look who's coming home for dinner

there he goes again
crawling around on all fours to create art
roll over expose your tummy
show me your TEETH
canines molars all of what can bite
porous unglazed china will never be the same after tonight

one handed tobacco rolling
charcoal black tip
sure are a talented one ain't ya
mean mugging the empty pack
till it's pissed enough to fight back
mad poet
sad poet
ashing on today's news
what can measure up to you
mad man
that poet
eccentric man
finger painting on my spine
dip your toes in second hand smoke
so i can eat your gun powder
load me up
shoot
splat on the window
another poem
penning another write
cheat codes to fill the pages
essence of your life

———————

Hope Soul is from Texas. Poetry is a way of life. Creating from all aspects of emotions. There is no other way
Allpoetry.com/Hope_Soul

[Marie-Jo Dorismond]

Adrift

I drift away, away
in the salty, open
azure sea.

I drift farther, farther
letting the waves
crest and crash.

I drift longer, longer
until the clamor and shouts
sound like distant murmurs.

I drift freer, freer
stretching out my arms
elevating my chest
and breathing with the sea.

MJ is a poet living in Los Angeles, California. She writes about the beauty of Haiti and its people. Allpoetry.com/Marie_J_Mond

[Alwyn Barddylbach]
Flowers in the Sun

'Я не блефую'

Moments lapse and reason dims,
the madman's words undone.
Clods of mud that fill my gut,
the senseless waste and terror,
a scent of things to come.

Scour the breathless sky, the seething sun,
clouds on fiery pillars bloom.
Flowers large as life bellow, billow, rogue,
brimstone scalding, demons scorching,
the bastard came and gone.

Flash of impotence possessed,
coward's folly, empires in the sun.
Spit and ash, shovel and crash,
blink an eyelid life unravels,
now put your glasses on.

These motherless Steppes he rides upon
in murderous fits of rage.
The manly thumps and metal chest,
into the pit that darkness scurries,
four billion years we'd come.

The moon because I pay to watch,
perpetual time ticks by. Beyond our seedless icy
fields the peerless stars which might have shone.
However brief and bright, upending pillars of light,
'not bluffing' however bright they shone.

Moments lapse, epiphany spins,
bastards blind and deaf are gone.
Clods of mud that fill my gut,
none that remember, none regret -
flowers in the sun.

_____

Putin's bluff and reign of terror goes nuclear - Is Life on Earth the only jewel in the crown to inherit the universe? Would anyone out there blink an eyelid if the lights went out? AB
Allpoetry.com/Barddylbach

[Rachel K. Martin]

White Eyeballs

white eyeballs glaring at me, dead
no life left to see air - - in the bed
trying to wonder if intelligence is seen
wondering who will care, not keen
they look bald and bold from a whore
to seem irate, no more
onto wondering why someone needs to handle them with gore
to hell -- widening the whites of the eyes shock with might
as the spirit from the body, lifted, pulled with fright
walking away to an unknown faded scene
drying on the bed, whites of the eyes' gooey pulp bubble from
pain, mean
the eyeballs' whites are at once expressionless
seeping to peak a glance, less and less
with the horrid, former world frozen in rubber, so plain
a color not loud, not to again, feign
the whites of the eyeballs
reflect the cold, white walls

―――――――――――

The poet's name is Rachel K. Martin. She graduated from Saint Louis University with a B.A. in English and from Webster University with a M.A. in Patent Agency. Allpoetry.com/BlueAngelIIII

[S. Libellule]

Memories

A faded picture in a locket
stray grey lint in my pocket
along with a torn ticket stub
to a place I'd long forgotten

A flash of your lost smile
that longest mile
to come tell you I was leaving
this playlist songs

Cataloguing all of these wrongs
which felt so right in that night

———————

Originally from New England, Libellule currently lives outside of Birmingham, Alabama. Poetic influences include Mary Oliver, Billy Collins and ee cummings.   Allpoetry.com/Little_Dragonfly

[Laura Sanders]

Mushroom picking in the 1970's

Bags soon filled up with nature's precious loot,
as us kids trudged around, in wet, black welly boots!
Searching for a sign of a white mark, or spot,
that would draw us in, so we could gather, the lot!

Dewy grass glistened, in a damp, dark earth.
Fungus spores offered rich pickings, at their birth.
Happiness and inner joy, as we picked away.
How gratifying, on this pre- Autumnal day!

Rounded, perfectly formed stems, pulled out, clean.
No maggots, or pitted caps, it was like a dream.
Wind smelt earthy, good, countryside fresh.
Mushroom fleshy, the aroma, we liked best.

Some grew near cowpats, others hid well in grass,
like a treasure- hunt, the hours minutes, passed...
Soon we dropped bulging bags inside.
Mum pleased, our little chests, swelled with pride!

My brother always spotted them, with his "eagle eyes".
He saw them from miles away, never failed to surprise!
We pulled the stalks from off of pink caps. Mum began
to fry chopped flesh, in her battered frying- pan.

You could live off the land, Dad said feeling merry,
on wild mushrooms, red Rosehip wine, juicy Blackberries.
But all this happened a long, long time ago,
Now there's no mushrooms ? Not even December snow?

I live in a beautiful part of the country, England and take inspiration from observing nature, people and animals. I enjoy writing all sorts of poetry . Allpoetry.com/Laura_Sanders.

[Lori Ann Berti]

Native Mountain

Tribute to the Native Americans

A hike ,A large mountain
No directions at hand
Wide river and many trees
Untouched virgin land.

Along a beaten path
Many tribes be forgotten
Foreigners leave painful wrath
Innocent corpses dead left rotten

Evidence from life that begun
Chants from a warrior chief
Headress under the sun
Following to his belief

I pick up an old stone
Three warped yet pointed edges
Overhead, an eagle had flown
Accross the mountain ledges

They worshiped mother earth
The Eagle ,the wolf , and the bear
Each named for their self worth
In thanksgiving we would share.

I see Women tend to their duties
I see Men eagerly hunt reckless
This mountains' natural beauties
I pick up an old beaded necklace

I watch the waterfall flow
As I begin to retire
A part of history I know
As rock and sticks light my fire

―――――――――

Lori Ann Berti is from Pittston Pennsylvania who is a Mom of 3 children and 2 grandchildren.I have been writing since the age of 12 and still learning more about the art of Poetry. Allpoetry.com/Lori_A_Berti

[Jennifer Bastedo]

Marvelous Picture Jasper

Marvelous marble mountain
True fountain
Cabin is certain woodsman talisman
Top of the mountain holy tree's
Is all he see's
Sitting in the breeze
Picture jasper
What a capture
Master of the inter fracture from along ago
Letting go is your flow
Rivers will glow

"You my Queen"

I am Jennifer Bastedo I am originally from New York, Long Island now living in Florida in my spare time, I like writing poetry I find it very therapeutic. Allowing myself to create and grow Thank you Allpoetry.com/Poetry_in_motion_soul

[Rachel K. Martin]

Always Amuses

water droplets washed my shoes
slippery their soles, from which water and dirt oozes
scurrying in them, dancing, jumping - - they have many uses
wet shoes in the rain, a trite heart always amuses

The poet's name is Rachel K. Martin. She graduated from Saint Louis University with a B.A. in English and from Webster University with a M.A. in Patent Agency. Allpoetry.com/BlueAngelιιιι

[Kayo Ono]

Nocturne

in the midd summer right around the Equator
night is still night wearing the deep black dress
galaxies are dancing on her soft hair
the moon was bitten a bit before the kiss

in the dark abyss of deep indigo sea
night is more night than ever we have seen
fluorescent jelly fishes, neon light coral trees
creatures are dancing like jelly beans

in the warm cozy place where we were
there was no light but just a happiness
talking laughing voice, hoping to remember
shower of the light, an exit button pressed

in the charcoal night, souls fly away
the world between visible and invisible
to find same colour of sparkles someday
Love we found, it's always so miracle

Pinky Promise is from Scotland, United Kingdom. A molecular biologist and a local music tutor for piano and violin. A small Succulent nursery owner. And Japanese mom of three children. Allpoetry.com/Pinky_Promise

[Maurice Hadley]

Feelings, thoughts and pains that haunt

The thoughts of being alone seep into my mind,
I look to my phone to begin the daily grind,
I have grown and I seek the answers I wish to find,
Or just to moan about the struggles that keep me behind.

The feelings of growing older with nobody to hold,
Some anxiety blowing in as I try not to fold,
I'm showing what I want to give but don't know if I can uphold,
My expectations are lowering day by day and yet untold.

The pain of losing has turned my skin thick,
It's all rather confusing I'm not even sure what makes me tick,
I'm still refusing what burned me and it damages the choices I pick.
For years myself I've been abusing hoping it would do the trick.

The past haunts me but the present is just as scary,
I go on late night jaunts but just find it to keep me wary,
Seeing what could be taunts but its unpleasant and never to the contrary
My heart flaunts but the feelings of pain that haunts my thoughts become my adversary.

———————

Poetry is something I am learning to deal with the trials and tribulations of life, It helps ease the anxiety by fueling my artistic venture. Allpoetry.com/Maurice_Hadley

[AJ Calvano]

Heartless

battling the cyan rain with a hole in my kingdom ~ heartless

feeling like Anakin, I panic, screaming nobody loves me
faded bruised and beaten into a deathbed of roses with thorns
combusting my lungs till broken
and the rain doesn't stop
it just beats like a damned beast forever chained in dead man's hand
perfect hell, an Italian hail of bullets tarnishing my dreams...
the moon looks really nice tonight ~
I wonder how it can be so cold yet so beautiful
then I look at me, a triple fish double moon
cancer, with no heat save the smoke hanging from my lips
God is crying for me
but I'm angry and yell back
"you never once had my back!"
all your most vile mistresses are drawn to me
used again by your wetness I can't find relief
I'm nothing, priceless to the efforts of my love

and yet it rains, slowing its pace to keep me from falling ill
I'm sorry

To be born human is to be born in this vast universe, in an isolated cell like planet inhabiting creative illusionists... O' but you can't fool a fool and the 5 W's and the H, offer no support.
Allpoetry.com/AJ_Calvano

[Bobbie Breden]

Up the Winding Road

Here I am again
Staring down a familiar
yet untraveled winding road
that stretches before me
365 brand new, untested
unexplored days
it's my own personal hillclimb,
my annual challenge

This time next year,
will I be looking at a trail of days
that were each filled with productive hours,
completed tasks, positive experiences,
accomplishments, aspirations realized,
a sense of purpose and direction,
treasured memories, timed well spent,

or will the path behind me
be littered with unfulfilled potential,
untried chances, unattempted opportunities,
hesitation, indecisiveness, irresolution, and
the empty hulls of the days
where time was squandered?

"Killing time" is a crime
that leaves no blood trail

and yet robs us of
a nonrenewable resource,
an invaluable finite asset

I will regard time
as a boon more valuable
than rare gems or precious metals,
a treasure of inestimable value
instead of regarding it
as my personal bottomless
piggy bank that I can loot
and swindle with impunity

Just as my body never forgets a calorie,
my lifetime never forgets a moment,
and if the skein of my life
is a tapestry that is woven daily
then it is up to me as the weaver
to make it worthy of tribute

a work of art filled with color,
celebration, and magic moments
and not a blank canvas
full of empty space

———————————

Retired Lady Leatherneck (US Marine), Renaissance woman, and a lover of life's mysteries. I'm interested in how others view the universe, and welcome opportunities to see it through their eyes. Allpoetry.com/Captain_B2

[Nadia Washington]

Down at the river

Streams, cobblestones, and mud - what is next?
Hidden beauty worth seeing.

Several secrets lie deep in the valley only plants can preserve. A wise sage moves forward; wisdom lies deep down. With its incomprehensible vastness, it gives clarity of mind and stillness.

Inky blackness

free gifts

livelihood.

Waterways are ever-changing.
Brown and white faces shine brightly while the incoming water carries them.

Babblers down the river were fascinated by just about anything burping, fluttering their chests with tales of riches. They did not miss a single frog or toad. A slingshot of mud filled their eyes and stained their brains, and merry-making

patter of

rabbits' feet

fondled their ears,

snapshot.

A tragic story of a man in severe distress floating in a swollen river of reflection, he took his life. The direct influence of the valley was visible in his fingers.

Witness of slaves and of freedom in its own growth, let us clap in the headwaters of forgiveness,
sis boom bah!

Bubble ohhh!

Slow down on the river!
It was my hope that I could contain my flow as I sat still and closed my curtains. I could only imagine touching the water. My identity is splintered by man-made structures.

I am Nadia Washington from Greenville SC, I am a business major college graduate and I enjoy writing and creativity because I believe there is beauty in everything even in unpleasant times. Allpoetry.com/Nadia_humanverse

[S. Libellule]

Memorie

More fragile than glass
as these years pass
etching their deep marks
signing my confessions

With so much again lost
at such a dear cost
this dwindling spindle
once more empties itself

Vain victories I did claim
things sorted by name
so randomly tossed
into disheveled drawers

While I try to make sense
of a melting past tense
that spills itself
more reckless than my ink

Leaves me doubting what is true
drowning in what is new
become deaf to the reverie
of what now escaped this memorie

Originally from New England, Libellule currently lives outside of Birmingham, Alabama. Poetic influences include Mary Oliver, Billy Collins and ee cummings. Allpoetry.com/Little_Dragonfly

[Irwin De Gannes]
Out Of Mind, Into Sight

In The Light Of Day, Next to Night
Into My Mind, Came A Fright
Out Of Mind, And Into Sight
The Joys Of Pleasures
Started To Bite...
They Nibble On: Lust; And Beauty
And Love; And Hope
The Pain Then Slowly... Overtook!
Memories Of Loves,
Once Lost And Found;
And Lusts! That seemed To Abound.
Flutters Like Beauty Out Of my Heart
Then When The Dark Of Night,
Stands Next To Day
The Joys Of Pleasures
Slowly... Went Away...
Out Of Mind, Into Sight
My Heart Stands Still
But Ceases Not!, To Hope...

Irwin De Gannes hails from the Caribbean Island of Trinidad and Tobago. I express high or low emotional periods of my life in Poetry, it preserves these moments in my life like a time capsule. Allpoetry.com/Irwin_De_Gannes

[Lorri Ventura]
(haiku)

If Heaven is real

It is filled with books and cats

And my mom lives there

―――――――――

Lorri Ventura is a retired special education administrator living in Massachusetts. Her writing has been featured in a number of publications. She has won three Moon Prizes for her poetry. Allpoetry.com/Lorri_Ventura

[April Hamlin-Sache]
Love Like Rain

When it's warm in my heart
whenever we are apart
I see a rainbow over my head
when I lie in bed.

I love you like no other
you are my favorite lover
my heart pours out to you like raindrops

I can't explain the power
I admire you like a flower
I recognize your love like raindrops

clouds spread apart
you are always in my heart
I never feel blue when surrounded by you

I feel fine as though you are still mine
love like rain all the time
love like rain
I cherish our time

I will never forget the years that you were mine
love the way you looked into my eyes
rubbed my hair
man, that was fly

You're so special to me
I keep reminiscing
remembering the time
the place

cannot forget the times I almost cried
when you left me behind
I guess you're in demand
you had other plans
that didn't include me
I'm not your only
because now you're married

when it rains it pours
well love is like that
sometimes love is a mystery like rain
because it sneaks up on you
some may say you never know when it's coming

I am originally from Indiana. I have 5 poetry books, 2 books of short stories and 7 series on amazon.com. I am a PT Receptionist and an Author/Writer. I love what I do!
Allpoetry.com/April_Sache

[Paul Crocker]

Who Took My Heart Away?

Do not look upon my face.
For I am not yours to be stared at.
I hear not what you speak whilst I dwell within this place.
Thoughts prevent my passing from this spot of which I am sat.
Why do you taunt me , wretch through my vulnerable demeanour?
The dark is not yours to bestow upon my flame.
Ember to ashes to dust shan't make these pastures greener.
Nor shall it keep such a ravenous beast tame.
May you bloody my face and dirty my hands.
Paint me in colours fraught with weakness and dread.
You tell me how it's to be, but I for one will not be damned.
This earth is disturbed yet I have not tread.
A shallow grave for a body of deep fragility.
Mourn me with sarcastic pity and spite.
It would be your only maskless ability.
Watching you incisively, cloaking my true feelings with the night.
Remember in detail how the warm blood fell drip drip drip.
Onto the concrete slab of the cold, unforgiving stone.
How my emotions were purposely ripped ripped ripped.
I wasn't left the decency of feeling alone.
Forgotten by tomorrow and not acknowledged by the stars.
Loveless and lifeless is how my body must lay.
Repainted with the history of my life's scars.
Where art thou foul bastard who took my heart away?

I am a poet from Bristol, UK. I started writing poems in 2001. I enjoy both reading and writing poetry and everything connected with it. Allpoetry.com/PoeticXscape

[Marta Green]
But You Said You Loved Me

But you said you loved me,
do you think I couldn't see?
I know her name is Claire,
she seemed to glow.

I am the sickest I've ever been, it is unfair,
and you tell me you are having an affair.
I am in the worst pain in my body, my mind,
you were the cruelest, not a piece of soul was kind.

In the hospital, I can plainly see,
how you never really loved me.
We wedded too young idealistic,
having babies in our lives was not realistic.

We had a messy divorce,
custody of your sons taken by force.
Child and spousal support I knew,
would be tortuous to you.

Regretting I spent fifteen years of my life,
with a man who ignored me with strife.
Here I lie on my bed of death extinguished,
saying good bye are my beloved sons, relinquished.

Marta Green is from the great state of Texas where she lives with her husband. She has three sons and 2 daughters. Her passion has always been writing, reading and art.
Allpoetry.com/Marta_Green

[Mia Emily]
that boy who swears by his wit, wisdom, and willpower

I know quite well, of a boy
from whom I learn
the ABCs of the Ws
joy from sorrow
the yesterdays and tomorrows

his acerbic wit
yet nothing compares
it hath no name
it holds no shame
love it hate it he couldn't care less
he is to his thoughts as food to life

he's naught but a lad
but boy has he gifted himself
some wrinkles spelt prudence
forgive him for flexing his wisdom
stretching an earshot to an hour-long walk
'cause next thing you know
you're awed by his flattering tongue

they say a man is but what he knows
he says a man is but what he does

life may try time and again
blessing in disguise many a time befall
he perfected the art of circumvention
behold, rise above he shall

standing tall with calculated mind
walking bold with decisive strides
he learnt well enough
to never walk the same route twice
for it's not the same footstep
nor does he the same boy

I know quite well, of a boy
from whom I learn
the this and that
but then again – all I have
is an infinity of time
what's another day, to learn a few more?

---

* Credits to The Darting Darling. Mia Emily is from the east coast of Malaysia. She is a professor at MARA University of Technology. She writes to express, not to impress, and is somewhat personal in her poetry work. Allpoetry.com/Mia_Emily

[Lockdown Larcs]
Walking The Wait

I waited (and waited)
for that someone
and nearly celebrated
but too soon they had gone

(I never knew why)

I walked (and walked)
seeking pastures new
then one day we talked
a destiny, I just knew

(I began to fly)

we danced (oh that dance)
for many a night
and soon a romance
blossomed into sight

(we saw eye to eye)

we kissed (oh that kiss)
could it last for ever
commit to this bliss
and regret never

(a knot we must tie)

a September (oh that September)
not a fall but our spring
always will I remember
the day my heart learned to sing

(now until we die)

_____

no wordsmith just an ordinary joe
see a reason & rhymes flow
things I couldn't see
until in lockdown 2020

AllPoetry a huge help in my book publishing
on amazon "One and All Rhymes Matter"

cheers LL Allpoetry.com/Lockdown_Larcs

[Andrew lee Joyner]
Life support

Tubes and wires keeping her alive,
Strands of doom, to be unplugged soon
Time is the enemy, stopping life inevitable
Unable to control, raindrops pour out of my eyes, each full of emotional webs; hard to let go
My love will never fade, It is unwavering
It seems so unreal, a horrible horrible nightmare
So broken inside but I must carry on
even though she's gone, she is still with me
Forever and always, I will never forget

———————————

Dedicated to my mother Tammy R.I.P 12/03/2022

I started writing poetry at a young age, it became a hobby of mine and now it's my life, I love to read and write. My inspiration is life, my sister is my muse Allpoetry.com/Andrew_Lee

[Ashley Vella]

Taunting Voices

Those tiny voices,
jolt me wide awake
taunting me, whispering,
Try and run,
from the damage,
this good - girl image
you've created,
is all a façade,
but the past
will catch - up
and on that day
all the cats...will be out of the bag.

AshVel is a 23-year-old aspiring poet from Malta. Thanks to poetry she discovered an outlet where to pour her heart out, and thus it's therapy to her. Allpoetry.com/AshVel

[Angel Williams]
the other father

Didn't love u until you got cancer but you were a father figure in my life and a good husband to mother but why no affection why no emotion why however you did with actions but i have to ask I'm an easy target I hurt easy and u knew how to do that very well emotionally and verbally why did it make u feel better did it give u power as a man I had to leave so you would stop but you always would say you are always welcome back never apologized for your wrongs but all is forgiven

―――――――――――

I am from Boston Mass I have been writing and publishing poems and have gotten awards off and on for 16 years I like sports and I am an animal activist from angel williams aka akster44 Allpoetry.com/Akster44

[Nick J. Vincelli]

channeling e. e. cummings

i i i i (& you you you you)
fly fly fly fly
seeing a C in the
sky sky sky sky
hearing(here-ing?)

~+~+~musical magicians~+~+~
&*&*& magical musicians &*&*&
symphonically scream:

the/el/le
//((((sky ▼ ✺ ‼ ✺ ▼ lord))))\\
cometh

BEhold/ware/wilder/stir!

i/t/he
i/me/my
tour
touring rolling (roiling trolling)
humorous/less jagged

w~~a~~v~~y
p-a-r-t-i-c-l-e-s

of/the/de
anti/ante luna(loony)-tics

dripping from Luna
(harsh mistress -/- mysterious harlequin?)
to the moon!
(bang--zoom!)

thy, thou & thee
beget savage slime
beating slimy time
(wounding all heels ←→ healing all wounds)

iMmmmmersed
in eh sea of luuuvvv

in ah ocean of
cHAOssHAOc

in au universe of
co-evolving convoluted
wOrDs

(dreaming of electric sheep dreaming of sheepish electrons:

[string of symbols, emoji, and multilingual glyphs]

(dreaming of electric sheep dreaming of sheepish electrons:

forever striving but
striving to forgo/et
the darkening of darkness
the brightening of brightness
the illumination of illusion

thusforth(ly):
the spirit of spurting
s+p!i#r!i#t!u?a+l:i^t$y
is hereby
re-solved!

&/or

forgotten−

_____

I'm a librarian and have been writing fiction and poetry (on and off) over the last 40+ years. My poems have been published in various anthologies. I currently live in North Carolina. Allpoetry.com/Tomcatx2021

[Jamal Mohammed Siddiqui]
Errors of Mankind

Oh man! What have you done to the Earth?
You turned the lands into the frightful fire.
You were on a mission to make this world a heaven
But in fact, you made it like hell
The soil that bloomed flowers of peace & calmness
But Loads of arms have made it a battlefield
Oh man! You have become the follower of your ego
Look! Because of your ego and arrogance
You have turned this earth into dreadful fire

Jamal Mohammed Siddiqui is from Hyderabad India. He is an International Author, Poet, Journalist, and LLB Graduate from London, England. Allpoetry.com/Jamal_M_Siddiqui

[Lisa F. Raines]

Arizona Sunset

Red Rock altars glow
Alive in the western sun

Canyons and buttes
The backdrop of Sedona

Mountains alive with vortexes
Signified by twisted tree trunks

Touching desert trees
I feel the Earth's power

Small piles of smooth rocks
Honor the shared energy

AlisRamie is from North Carolina, USA.
Interests include: philosophy, history, international relations, politics, poetry, art, design, jazz, funk, and some good old soul.
Allpoetry.com/AlisRamie

[Douglas R Colthurst]

A Focus in Fluidity

Those eyes
bind me,
hold me,
scold and
nurture me.

Fragile yolks
that don't
quite tear,
but tear
the edges
of my world.

The endless
essences
of those
before.

Irises of eyes
with containment
masquerading
as contentment.

Will
I enter?
Cross such threshold
of Medusal variance?

What chalk mark
shall I be
on her wall
of iniquity?

Ah, Chaos.
How tempting
to enter
your wild entropy.

Oh,
to walk this life
an empty husk
to exist beyond
my physical frail.

Her eyes
now have me.
Include me.

As I become
a part of
her coalescing
dance of ecstasy.

Born small town, central Illinois. (350) Educated U. of Illinois, Urbana-Champaign, BS U. of Illinois Dental College DDS. Love writing, painting, cooking, music ,wine, Harley
Allpoetry.com/Victortouche

[Saffron E Morris]

Poetic Passion

Words drip in pain
painting the canvas
with colours of suffering.

Letters doused in rage
fuel the flames
igniting my inspiration.

Words grip, caress wounds
and wholly consume me
bending my pen
with the weight of
each verse.

Laying wakeful in
dead of night
a victim of words
frolicking and breeding
rejecting sleep.

Blood-soaked thoughts
smear the page
in shades of regret.

Worst fears bleed like
ink upon pallid sheet

sentences spill
stripping mask
exposed -
my weaknesses.

S. E. Morris is 24 years old and from south Wales. Writing is how she bears the brunt of life.

Allpoetry.com/Pennyforyoursoul

[Michael A. Mannen]

King of the snow

The king of the snow comes and proposes a snowstorm. He offers sentiments to the surroundings:

"Early ice wind and, so faintly the snow goes down
Pearl leaf is the silver frost of the flower
with the frost color of snow sorrow,
and the green will stay there after.
nothing more first frost only so an echo"

Michael Mannen is a writer based in Kentucky and a graduate from the Harvard School of Public Health. Allpoetry.com/diamondstoo1

[Bobbie Breden]

Lost in Le Louche

The sun has retired, eventide descends
Blessed darkness, the dominion of the fairies
He seeks the beryl fairies, glowing emerald green

He strolls the streets of the Vieux Carré
His feet traveling the familiar Bourbon Street pavement
To Jean Lafitte's and his nightly tryst with Le Louche

With a familiar wave to the barman, Lucien,
He wanders up the stairs, seeking his favorite balcony
The balcony that used to be their meeting place

She waits at the table for him, his escort
His companion in the green hour each night
She awaits, his guide within his verdigris dreams

He hopes tonight, as he does each night,
That the Pontarlier glass and engraved silver brouilleur
Will relieve the anguished longing and loneliness

For each evening, he would sit at this table
Across from his beautiful Marie, his beloved wife
The angelic woman he would spend his eternities with

Destiny and yellow fever destroyed his dreams of their future
And now each night, wandering lost between two worlds
He seeks the radiant abyss in the aphrodisiac of the self

Green Dreams are his refuge now, a bit of magic in a glass
Lost in Le Louche, the heavenly devil's brume in a beaker
He spends his nights in an exquisite hell of his own design

The dewy cold hits the absinthe, the liquore's essential oils escape
Now Le Louche appears, a spontaneous cloudy opaline emulsion
Awakening and welcoming the juices of which she is made

He gazes mesmerized at the bottle and the Pontarlier glass
Remembering the reflection of the glass in her absinthe eyes
He would lose himself in those once rapturous eyes, now gone

He imagines he hears a voice so familiar, like a voice in dream
The rustle of her gown as she swept across the floor to join him
Once the sweetest and gentlest of creatures, his heartbreak is complete

Now he gazes at the blue blossom that arises from the sugar
The absinthe alight in an indigo inferno, his private purgatory in a glass
A rare incandescent spirit, passing through every shade of opal

And the consecrated liquore becomes his liberation, his deliverance
In that instant bringing acquiescence to his head, acceptance to his heart
Once one of New Orleans' artistic luminaries, now just a disconsolate recluse

Another night immersing his pain in the enigmatic viridian elixir
Another night of watching the alchemy of water and fire together
Transform shades of malachite and jade into opal and pearl

Amid the banal, inconsequential comings and goings of the masses
He watches the flow of humanity on the streets below and sighs wearily
As the tranquil absinthe waits for him to lose himself yet again...

In the ritual of Le Louche

Retired Lady Leatherneck (US Marine), Renaissance woman, and a lover of life's mysteries. I'm interested in how others view the universe, and welcome opportunities to see it through their eyes. Allpoetry.com/Captain_B2

[William E Roberts]
A portrait of me

Collodion:
Am I a man, or am I a boy?
Sixteen years, empty in my portrait
Left arm rested, unnaturally posed
My confidence is an anchor
Will my ship ever set sail?
Toiling at the mill, twelve hour days
Uneducated, ignorant, useless machine
Low society, dirty and unattractive
How long can I exist without ever living?
A slave to my standing, inescapable dread
Constricted and smothered by my heritage
Life is unfair, I once had so many dreams
Adventures, travels, life, love, happiness
But I'm trapped in this mill, life's unfulfilled A somber existence,
I'm a boy in a portrait

Ambrotype:
I'm not a boy, I am a man
Sixteen years, filling my portrait
Right arm posed, its strength apparent
Confident in my, undying work ethic
My ship will sail soon, in a fortnight I leave
I've toiled long enough, down at the mill Experience my
education, graduating soon
On the deck of a whaler, classes are equal

I'm going to feel life, I've outgrown existing
Be a slave to my dreams, chained lovingly
Breathe in salty air, exhale discrimination
This life is my book, I will write the ending
My dreams are reality, adventures to come
I've escaped the mill, pursuing life and love
Joyously embracing, that man in a portrait

Experiences so vast
Getting older so fast
An outlet that lasts
For thoughts I cast
Allpoetry.com/Unexpected_Bill

[Sean Cooke]

Autumn Leaf

I watched the Autumn leaf float with the winds blow.
It's time to move on it's time to let go.
I smell the Autumn and feel the change in me.

The summer skin I've shed.
Now it's time to look ahead.
Prepare for what life brings.

An open door.
A new road.
A candle to light my way.

I am an Autumn leaf.
Gliding through life.
Feeling the vibration of a moment in time.

I am a 32 year old man from northern England, reading and writing poetry is now a satisfying and productive part of my life. I thank my mother and father deeply and all those who read my poetry. Allpoetry.com/Arsenalfan30

[Brian Shaun Watson]

A Beautiful August Day

A cool breeze blowing
the green leafy tree
and a cloudy sky.

My Name is Brian Shaun Watson And I am from Nashville, Tennessee. I was born in Hampton, Virginia on Friday, August 11th, 1978. I've been reading and writing since I was 10 years old. Allpoetry.com/Brian_S._Watson

[Kelsey Jean]

Sunrise

My eyes awaken as dark night fades.
I dotingly cradle you in cozy slumber.
The warmth of your skin invigorates my senses.
Your chest rises and falls like stars once in the sky.
Daylight seeps in as your silent body rouses.
Lush scent imbues like dew on blades of morning grass.
Your lips whisper their last sweet dreams.
Revitalized mind returns to state of activation.
A smile welcomes as dust shakes from rested eyes.
A new day has emerged.
Another blackness turned and you're here with me.
Never has sunrise looked as beautiful.

Kelsey Jean is from Owatonna, Minnesota. Being a mother of 2 beautiful daughters, 15 years providing adult disability care, and the love of an incredible man offers an endless supply of inspiration. Allpoetry.com/Kelsey_Jean

[TS Darling]
Storm

I watched the rain last night
Watching as it performed
I thought, 'How brave the rain,
To jump from clouds roaring'
Falling to dance in sight
To splash and then reform
I thought, 'How kind the clouds,
To spark night with lightning'
Crashing into mountains
To light up the dark sky
I thought, 'How can I join,
To splash around dancing?'
How might I take that flight?
Then thought, 'You are my storm

'

_____

'You have a magnificent quality in you to find beauty in the most awful, boring, and shittiest things.' - My Ex
Allpoetry.com/T.S._Darling

[Patricia Marie Batteate]
Do You Remember

Remember the days of penny candy
A three cent glass of lemonade
Remember learning to ride a bike
When allowance was earned and saved

Remember catching frogs at the pond
Building a fort in the backyard
Remember when the house was unlocked
Where the family dog stood guard

Remember when dinner was called
The family all ate together
Remember waiting for your birthday to come
How the year took forever

Remember the first day of school
Holding your parents' hand
Remember reciting the pledge of allegiance
Where In class, we all would stand

Remember your very first kiss
How the world seemed anew
Remember mom at your bedside
The times you had caught the flu

Remember obeying your parents
Respecting our elders was the rule
Compassion for people we felt
Making fun of was considered cruel

Remember how you thought
You had it all figured out
And now that you've grown up
You have nothing but doubt

_____

I am a 7th generation Californian. I am an engineer, poet and artist. 'Tolerance is a gauge used to determine just how much a person is willing to put up with'

Allpoetry.com/Patricia_Batteate

[Rachel K. Martin]

The Bee and The Hummingbird

Pardon me, Mr. Bee
I have come to get some nectar, honey!
No, you see, Mr.Hummingbird, see me
I have been here since half-past-three
No mind, Mr. Bee, this flower belongs to me
Actually, Mr. Hummingbird, the flower always belongs to the honey bee
Look here, pal! I've been here since half-past-three!
buzz-off! or I'm gonna give you a whack times three!
Oh! Mr. Hummingbird I am scared of thee
but I have to say, shyly
that flower belongs to the honey bee
we'll have to share or I'll put you in a snare!
alright,. that sounds fair
a peck for you from your beak
and a peck from me from this stinger, bleak!
I think I stung you with my stinger, gee!
- - and down went Mr. Hummingbird and Mr. Bee
to the ground, both feeling a little dizzy
while along came a little girl to decree,
"that this was my Daisy!"
she picked the flower, yellow and brown
the hummingbird and the bee sat and watched with a frown
as the girl walked away she pointed at another daisy for the day
both the hummingbird and the bee did not despair, neither did

stay
they both flew quickly away
afraid of another fray
and come what may!
the hummingbird and the bee were happy!
as you can see not sharing last time, got them no honey, no honey
this is a little lesson on learning to share,
there is always enough of plenty to spare
actually, there were plenty of daisies, in the field, over there
and everywhere and everywhere
just beside and many more
daisies and daisies, by and by, galore!
the bee and the hummingbird learned that setting pride aside
it won't get wide and snide
as the hummingbird and the bee
flew around the daisies happily and

_____

The poet's name is Rachel K. Martin. She graduated from Saint Louis University with a B.A. in English and from Webster University with a M.A. in Patent Agency. Allpoetry.com/BlueAngelıııı

[Bobbie Breden]
Painful in Pink ~~ Free Verse

Inspired by sarcasm, contempt, spite, insolence, snarkiness, and survivors of bullying everywhere...

Lovely little girls, petite perspicacious predators
Pint-sized, ponytailed, pink, prepubescent, predacious
Diminutive deliverers of deliberate destruction
They reveled each time another's spirits are shattered

Silver-tongued savvy socialites, stylish and sought after
Self-appointed summit of the school's social strata
Puberty's popularity pivotal pinnacle
Incendiary snarkiness, weapon of choice

Estrogen raptors, self-possessed pyromaniac princesses
Détente with the dejected and downtrodden doubtful
Debased, defamed, disparaged, detracted
Order of the day, excoriate the innocent, vilify the virtuous

Gullible girls, guileless ground zero for guerilla tactics
Naïve nerds never knowing what hit them
Main event for merciless mean girls' more often than not
Student aristocracy makes bullying bookworms a brutal bloodsport

Sharp tongues skewer shy, sheepish, self-effacing students
Seldom safety in numbers, more nerds equals more targets
But brave adult no more to stand idly by when victims are chosen
Because bruised and beleaguered inner child remembers

Retired Lady Leatherneck (US Marine), Renaissance woman, and a lover of life's mysteries. I'm interested in how others view the universe, and welcome opportunities to see it through their eyes. Allpoetry.com/Captain_B2

[Haze Le'Shay]

Loving You

If loving you was a pill
I'll take you endlessly
Admiring you is a drug I'll ne'er quit taking
If adoring you acquire me to the moon
Then I'll ne'er say cease
Your love gets me weak
It's something I'll forever seek
Through healing and tears
I'll fight to keep adoring you
From your body to the soul
I'll never stop searching you
If loving you expresses happiness
Then I'll perpetually seek your love
Finding you is all I need
Because I was all I need

Hello, I'm Haze. I'm from Lake Charles, Louisiana. I reside in Houston, Texas. Ever since middle school, I enjoyed writing. All poetry helps me get things out that I could never speak. Allpoetry.com/doseofhaze

[Annabelle Molyneux]

US Army

You were there when at times
I was irrational
You loved me so much
That I, your wife, am just a little bit deranged
And I love you even more,
Afraid of your temper.

You gave your all to the marriage
And I thought that you being strict, that you were abusive
You were not
You were a captain in the military
When you say that in the army, it was a shit-shower-shave in 5 minutes,
You expect me to follow that
Because you want the best for me
To be like a soldier
Because life is tough.

You were like my family
I didn't know why they had to be so strict with me
But because I am their daughter
They wanted me to be straightened out.

But I, your companion, treat you like a king
Because my love for you is eternal
Despite the scars

You were not abusive when I thought you were
You were a soldier
In uniform.

Annabelle Molyneux is from Salt Lake City, Utah. She is originally from the Philippines and immigrated to the USA in 2009. Annabelle is married to Max Allen Molyneux of Winnebago, Minnesota. Allpoetry.com/Annabelle_Molyneux

[Lorri Ventura]
(haiku 2)

The Christmas tree tilts

Ornaments fly through the air

Where could our cat be?

———————

Lorri Ventura is a retired special education administrator living in Massachusetts. Her writing has been featured in a number of publications. She has won three Moon Prizes for her poetry. Allpoetry.com/Lorri_Ventura

[Mary L. Steffen]

dinosaur dance

dinosaur dance
beyond the world of good
tomorrow search

I am a retired Nursing assistant. Live in rural Iowa . Have been married for 36 years with two full grown sons.
Allpoetry.com/Hawkeyes

[Bobbie Breden]

the existential parade

to exist

born in a thicket of obfuscation
life is risk against certainty
ancestors that howl dark tales

the tyranny of conscious thought
the monsters of the mind
with dry and brittle souls

fields greener in their description
than in their actual greenness, verdigris
in all its shades and hues beyond your reign and relm

the devil rides a full moon
the wind, biting to the bone
time rushes by, love rushes by, life rushes by

all the hearts of the earth will love and be lost
touch is lethal, it leaves one's heart at the mercy of another's
fate is inexplicable and without compassion

we travel between eternities
connected by an endless ribbon of emotions
emotions searching for the words that would set them free

to live

the sounds of the night
carried on a breeze as gentle
as the breath of a fairy

silently, in the trough of the wave
brilliantly, in the seconds after lightning's flash
expectantly, in the moments of silence before music

the earth is motionless
and the universe rotates around it
waiting with no end in sight

suddenly in that moment
i feel as if i can hear the earth
breathing beneath me

i listen, and the wind is full of voices,
of ancient nights, and distant music
the world is full of all manner of mysteries

life is covered with veils of wonder
and walking through life backwards
ensures that one will miss the adventures ahead

to love

we cling to memories as if they define us
but what we do defines us and i have my truth to tell
truth, that you don't know all of me yet

the truth is that you are the wonder of my life
your heart beats fiercely, mine just ticks
and i have not gifts to offer such a wonder

save to share the simple pleasures of life
if you are hungry i will feed you
if i am mad, you will tell me

we learn to live above our demons
and you're going to be the one
the one who saves me, frees me

you have given me to know that i have not misread
your soft caring heart, so you have my loving thoughts,
and where you have my thoughts, there you also have me

love that is not truthful is not love, it is passion
love that has no passion is soulless
you are my truth, my love, my passion, my soul

Retired Lady Leatherneck (US Marine), Renaissance woman, and a lover of life's mysteries. I'm interested in how others view the universe, and welcome opportunities to see it through their eyes. Allpoetry.com/Captain_B2

[Lisa F. Raines]
Young Graduate

Think through thoroughly
Every move you make,
BEFORE you make it

Love passionately your person,
Everyone needs one

Cry when you're happy,
Laugh when you are sad

Keep things in perspective,
Especially your time
And your money

Always find the context
Of every situation

Study history, and the historian,
Art, as well as the artist

Develop an ethical code,
And live by it

Protect the people in your life

Believe deeply in what you believe

And never lose hope—
Remember,
This too shall pass

So take notes

AlisRamie is from North Carolina, USA.
Interests include: philosophy, history, international relations, politics, poetry, art, design, jazz, funk, and some good old soul.
Allpoetry.com/AlisRamie

[Erica Byrne]

Seeing of truth

looking into the eyes of a stranger
As the walls are closing in
Seeing a reflection of myself
My eyes are deeper with confusion
Never comprehending why that is
As something reminded me of who I am
Contemplating through each reasons
Nothing seems wrong or right
Just a feeling at the pit of my stomach
Teaching me that the feeling for me is right
Its never the knowing in your mind
It is the feeling that is inside my gut
Looking into the mirror as I became clear
Never be the same as the fear is increasing
The strength is what grew stronger
Showing me it is ok to be a new me

I have been writing since I was 12 years old and now I am 30. I have one book out called thoughts, feelings, goofiness and looking into getting my next poetry book published Allpoetry.com/EricaByrne92

[Paula Rowlands]

Your Show

Don't let the Ultracrepidarian
Ruin your day
Don't let them bamboozle you
In to thinking their way

Let the snollygosters
Unravel in time
Blockstacles will fall
They'll pay for their crime

You keep on shinning
Let your splendor glow
Forget all the derelicts
This is your show!

———————

Pivotal Poetry is a poet from Western Australia who enjoys beautiful spring days and being lost in the magical world of poetry at night. She also enjoys writing her poetry blogs to inspire others. Allpoetry.com/Pivotalpoetry

[Dr. Michelle Wendy Hacker]
In Pursuit of the Lyrical Life

The music in this house
has changed a bit of late.
With my sweet wife's passing,
lyrical tunes went as
well; those mild
pianissimo melodies
broken with rhapsodic
giggles and fair laughter.
The expressive sounds of
small murmurs with little
muses of hummed tunes
drifting from room to room
without her legato
movements throughout the day.
that lyrical music has gone as well.

With Mom's arrival
comes a percussiveness
with crashing cymbal sounds
and pizzicato speech
punctuated by a
laughing cacophony..
A stadium roaring
has come to roost with me
and follows me throughout
the house, echoing out
to the garden with, great

thunder sheets, bellowing;
this guest has drummed out all
known musical structures
and the need for scoring
any notes on the page.

Thank God for the forest
and the silence of the
tall trees, where I can still
recall a Borodin
melody and soothe this
seemingly ragged heart.
The whispering of trees
make new lyrical sounds
unlike any other
music I have written
or heard, and I thank this
noisy guest, for the found
poignant reminder, that
all music comes from here
amongst the singing trees,
within the seeking heart,
and cannot be so quelled
when the lyrical life is sought.

I was born in Chicago in 1955. I am the author of several fictional novels and three books of poetry. I currently live in Hendersonville, NC, just outside Asheville. I am recently retired. Allpoetry.com/Michelle_Ende

[Tor Arne Jørgensen]

Footprints on broken paths

Thick trunks
are weighed down
by age.
White cliffs
finds rest
from the blistering sun.

A meadow of flowers
quietly sleeping.
A moon is greying
against the night.

Thoughts
are summoned.
The ocean
makes its peace.

Timeless eyes
are fading away.

As these lives are now coming to life.

I am the father of 2 boys aged 12 and 14, I am married to my wife of 23 years. I come from Norway and live just outside a town called Grimstad in a small villa called Fevik.
Allpoetry.com/Jørgensen

[Stephanie Campbell]

My Body Yet No Longer My Choice

When I discovered that you were slowly growing in my tummy
I can't lie I wept, and I felt absolutely crummy
How could I let this happen, knocked up by another looser
The day I told him, was the last day he was my abuser
You helped me free myself from his lethal grasp
He claimed I was just trying to trap
As if he was a magnificent man, honorable by far, maybe only in his mind
This I could never have opined
As you grew I fell in love with you enjoying your tiny movements
Who knew you would arrive after only 5 months
I was starting to get excited, overjoyed at the thought of you
Even your dad smiled when he found out you were a boy getting protective as my belly grew
Sadly my joy short lived, as the Doctor did your first sonogram
He said it appears that you may have passed from what he can see from the exam
But new state laws forbid him from removing your corpse from my abdomen
That there are still signs of life, possibly some motion
Forced to birth you, broke me, left me obliterated
How could I have prepared for what would eventually leave me debilitated
My little Angel Noah, I couldn't bare to let go of your lifeless body, you fit in the palm of my hand

Being forced to give birth to my child whom had passed is something some will Thankfully never understand
Yet they get to "Vote" on whether or not a woman should ever have to go through such pain
How is that even remotely humane ?
My precious little Angel, Noah Christopher
I pray losing you will prevent other Mothers from having to suffer

———————

I'm from San Bernardino, C.A.. I started writing poetry as a way to express myself and my emotions, because often when I would try speaking my feelings I was at a loss for words.
Allpoetry.com/SCampbell

[Alessandro Chimienti]

Your Caress

If I ever loved,
and ever moved so delicately,

as a drop of rain
that steals the colors,

then my heart, a lie
my desire, a curse.

My thoughts of you,
invisible broken glasses,
sharp, cutting through my despair.

And your simple elegance,
close to perfection,
that pierces through my veiled faith.

Only a whisper left,
and a sweet word,
grace.

Alessandro was born in Italy and currently lives in Los Angeles. His infinite and desperate love for a beautiful woman he saw only once from afar, gently protects him from pain through poetry. Allpoetry.com/Alinooo81

[S. Libellule]

Unforgotten

All the things I recall
are still faded leaves of fall
painted in watercolor
left out in the rain

As if seen through a tear
with some facets still clear
as a precious gem
these keepsakes I reclaim

What then to cherish
which memories to let perish
on the dulling pyre
of ever-fading embers

So many days I did live
still somehow able to give
each of them a name
each a most treasured place

But now the days dwindle
by the Fates with their spindle
not a single thing now regrettable

with this one life... unforgotten

Originally from New England, Libellule currently lives outside of Birmingham, Alabama. Poetic influences include Mary Oliver, Billy Collins and ee cummings.   Allpoetry.com/Little_Dragonfly

[Sherin Dawn]

My Crescent of Happiness

When I see the smile of my kid
I see the crescent of my Happiness
The light that falls on my face
Cooling the deep sea of sadness

Wiping down my streams of grief
In your eyes my dear i see
The ocean of love and joy
Spreading all over as you smile
Giving a meaning to all that I feel
I Feel the pain increase a mile

Oh... please smile to me...my child
Just give a reason to this wild
Come and hold me to your life
Protect me from this knife
That's taking away my joy
Judging me as a coy..
Feeling surreal I say
Hope all of this will pay
For to Almighty I turn
Pray that He sees my prayer in return....

Sherin Dawn hails from Thrissur, Kerala, India.
Ever since I was a Kid, I loved Poetry, prose and reading.
I wrote My first poem when I was 7yrs.
Poetry helps me to express my Feelings and emotions.
Allpoetry.com/Shescherry

[Nadia Washington]

Silk web of the star-lit night

The Holy Spirit filled the mulberry sky with sweet-fair and grace. As a fabric of life, Mary, Jesus, and the butterfly race are a mellowing force that mellows us like a sweet odour. Fire howls from an airy vision with a silver-clad belly, bringing rivers of freedom.

In the calm of midnight, silkworms churned in the spinners' work, and drops of servitude adorned the room.

A blanket of softness was woven from the sounds of rain to wrap and shepherd the baby. So, on that starlit night, the King of Kings was born under the shield of silkworms. They kept the beat and let their fibers tell a greater story for all to see.

I am Nadia Washington from Greenville SC, I am a business major college graduate and I enjoy writing and creativity. Allpoetry.com/Nadia_humanverse

[Harrison Green]
Special Catch

There is a fine line between love and sadness
One does not come without the other
You cannot fear sadness and welcome love

We are told that there are other fish in the sea
But what about your special catch?
The only person that can tell you everything will be okay and you'll believe it?

Love can change
But like matter it cannot be destroyed
By choice or by accident, there will always be a place in your heart for your special catch

The great thing about love is it is spontaneous
You don't see it coming
But you get to experience the rush you get from it

"I already had my first love"
A common misconception told by teenagers
Told before they even reach the tenth grade

Your special catch will redefine your definition of love
They will make you feel like your life has led up to one singular moment to this point
All for the rest of your life to be centered around them

We don't get to pick and choose between sadness and love
We don't get to choose the person that brings either one of them
But we do get to decide how much effort we will put in to keeping
Our Special Catch

Poetry gives me a way of describing my emotions that others won't understand. Any relating my feelings to things current in the world, I feel a deeper connection to my work.
Allpoetry.com/Harrisonagreen

[S. Libellule]

Memory..

It is an old pocket watch
ticking off and on
engraved and embossed
to tell the good times
but with an old brass chain
once fastened to your vest

now only to my sorrow

_____

Originally from New England, Libellule currently lives outside of Birmingham, Alabama. Poetic influences include Mary Oliver, Billy Collins and ee cummings. Allpoetry.com/Little_Dragonfly

[Amathaunta Creator]
Last Meltdown... Reincarnation

We are here together at this time
this time
this very time

Let us embrace each other
till the coming end come for us

Hold me even tighter than before
I want to remember this till out next reincarnation

I will not care when we are reborn & your married, engage or
living a living an denigrate lifestyle
I will find you and make your life right again

Even by chance

If you were born the same sex as me
It matter not to me
Our souls will connect once again

We are embracing each so tightly
Our last heat exchange between us is lustrous

I wonder if this is true love
Were both crying like angels

Banish for our unspeakable love

The fire surround us
This is the end
Let us kiss one last time before we are reborn

I truly love you

————————

A lifeform that aspires to something beyond human understanding.. I wake up and look out the window and I wonder what should I do.
I don't know how to do much and will never be special to anyone's heart...
Allpoetry.com/Amathauntacreator

[Emma Ryan]

Pathological Liar

A web of words, a tangled vine
I weave with practiced ease
A truth half-told, a blatant lie
I speak with perfect ease

My words are weapons, sharp and sly
I wield them with precision
I hurt those close to me, and why?
My affliction's decision

I see the hurt in eyes that trust
And yet I cannot stop
The urge to bend the truth to must
To make my reality hop

I am a thief, a fraud, a cheat
A master of disguise
I am a liar, incomplete
A victim of my lies

But deep inside, I long for true
To be free from this disease
To find redemption, start anew
And live a life with ease

I really read Homer, not Voltaire
I really went out with three people, not two
I really wrote in green ink, not blue
I cannot explain why I lie to you

I illustrate my weekend in color, not dark
I read beautiful words that were never actually for me
I stoically played the victim, when I wasn't, and I hid when I was
So why do I feel safer in this "fake me?"

I really skipped lunch, not forgot food
I really scored three times, not four
I really hid in the darkness, not slept
And yet, these lies, I sell more

I hide behind this beautiful broken girl that I'm not
I cannot face the boring, breaking girl that I am
Lies were the ways I made my own truth, I thought
But when light is shed, I feel like the lamb

The lamb on the alter
Waiting
For the blade
For the spear
For the sharp steak
For something to stab me
Or stop me
Somehow

But it doesn't come
The sheet of my truth that I sewed out of white lies
Has torn
And ripped
With a bloody gash
And I am exposed
But not dead
Because they are better than I am
They are purer than I am
They won't hurt me the way that I have hurt them
With the comfortable truth
That wasn't the truth at all

Just let me be alone
Or hide behind that sheet
Behind that person I made

I'm comfortable there
Even if it is wrong
That lie is the best truth I've found
Because it is my own
Because it is mine
Because I am finally in control

Emma is currently a sophomore in high school who spends her free time advancing her writing skills and has a love for literature. Allpoetry.com/Emma_Ryan

[Madilyn Sulda]
Red Roses

He made me feel love
when he gave me
the bouquet of red roses.
My cheeks flushed
the same shade of red,
as the roses in my hand.
I gave him my heart
the way he gave me the bouquet,
with such grace and care.

He traced my fragile heart
the way I traced the delicate petals,
of the red roses
that were placed so perfectly,
as I saw our love.

His tempting words
lured me down a treacherous path
that went past the surface
of the love I was used to.
When I touched
the hidden thorn on the rose,
he showed me his true intentions.
The thorn punctured deep into my skin.
He punctured deep into my heart.

Blood trickled down my finger.
Teardrops trickled down my face.

His betrayal was unexpected,
like how getting pricked by a rose thorn
can be really unexpected.
He left me devastated,
because I thought our love was flawless,
like the bouquet of red roses
he so innocently gave me.

―――――――――

A writer from Bernardston, Massachusetts. Poetry is one of my favorite ways to express my ideas and emotions! Allpoetry.com/madilyn.s

[Stewart Brennan]
To Wear the Mask of the Dead

Stand and deliver e.e. cummings, though you know me not,
steadfast through the days of yore,
days which have passed before.
Black n whites, where eyes were shot,
or has whiskey then forgot.
A toast to you and anti-war,
service in ambulance corps,
though three months in prison fraught,
the enormous room then wrought.
I look back from foreign shore,
ponder writing all the more,
regardless of critics caught,
and the demons that are fought,
with many things I abhor.

_____

Stewart Brennan is a Poet on AP with a penchant for writing on nature, the human condition, economics and politics. He is also the author of 3 books called "The Activist Poet" (Vol 1, 2 & 3) Allpoetry.com/Minstral

[Glenn Houston Folkes]
Don't Forget

My memory is lost in a dream, yet still,
I have my coffee by the windowsill,
The dew on the glass and the chill in the air,
They remind me I have to go somewhere,
Thank God, I have my car keys on hand,
I always forget them and ruin my plans.

I am a lover of the arts. Although this poem was written when I had my car, I am a pedestrian and thespian, still, I am not a lesbian. I write poetry for fun and for my artistic endeavors. Enjoy. Allpoetry.com/Barkdream69

[Sharon Diaz]

Ode to 'My Loose Woman'

Exuberant, a glorious adamant presence
I found my younger self browsing through the metaphors
and imagery of a loose woman, undressing right before my eyes,
Layer after layer she showed me the most infamous judgments-
Woman, my loose woman,
I carry your blooden epithets
announcing the rebirth of my clandestine cavalry-you said
We are the ladies of Kalo; machas, unhitched from truism-
Little by little I watched you crown in my entrails-
the roots of my revolution carving themselves, alone-
As I fell in love with the untested, precarious womb of her-
Woman, my loose woman-
Volatile and unguided, erratic to love-
And to be loved-genderless, promiscuous-
You said-upset the natural order, I will guide you-
As the roots entangle me, I surely made love to you-perhaps I still am-
As I orgasmically rise from your arms, I've now become-
A loose woman...my own loose woman

My Loose Woman is a song by Sandra Cisneros.

Sharon was born and raised in Puerto Rico. Lives in the Sunshine State of Florida. She is an English professor, beach enthusiast, and animal lover. For her poetry is 'the rhythm of life'.
Allpoetry.com/Norahs_Zaid

[Moss M.Jacques]
Our Story

I'm a secret lover
Who can't resist taking his secret
To the whole world.
Forever love
Bestows on my childhood memories
A kind of unknown language
That you can't talk
But you can only feel it,
illuminates the dark side of the moon
into a giant harvest of light,
Cheerful, but yet unaccustomed.
Hawaii, paradise of love
Here I come excited and unafraid
I will bring my love
Make me a paradise.
Ephemeral and shattered
The storyline doesn't match
My true story.
Don't cry for me.
Misleading and disharmonious,
The storytelling doesn't tell
The whole story
Cry me a river.
This is how the story goes
Secret lover no more

I don't trust myself around you
But I trust you blindly
To map out the rain
In a foggy and cloudy sky
Together
Our story is one and unbreakable
Forever love
In a foggy and cloudy sky.

———————————

Moss M. Jacques is the recipient of many literary prizes in his early twenties both in France and the US. Poetry, his first love, allows him the freedom to search for a reference point.
Allpoetry.com/Moss_M._Jacques

[Garnet Goode]

Lost and Found

A Forest Bathing Experience

Scents bring me back to childhood
Campfire, falling leaves, wet wood

Colours of leaves with trees bending to light
Calm rushes over, knowing the future is bright

Patterns in bark, moss on ground
Fungus on trees, can't hear a sound

Taking in sights, sounds, and fresh air
Breathing, serine, texture, self-care

Admiring the forest for the trees
Learning togetherness, one finally sees

Climbing another hill but need to be humble
I could slip and fall, my life could crumble

Light dancing amoungst the trees
Feel my higher power, drop to my knees

Mud on shoes, pants look rough
Finally learning; don't sweat the small stuff

Walk comes to an end but my journey's just beginning
No place for ego, complacency or sinning

Forgetting the past or worrying about the future
Living in the present; healing wounds with love and suture

Smells, sights, touch and sound
I was lost but now I'm found.

───────────────

Garnet started writing poetry as a coping mechanism during recovery from alcohol dependency. He is enjoying his sobriety and love for poetry. Allpoetry.com/Garnet_Peirson

[Matthew Broughton]

Memories of You

Swimming into the void
everything dying, falling apart
We had an unstable start
We love the feel
of each other's heart
My heart is filled with love
by the mention of your name.
The sight of you does things to me
I am never able to explain
The thought of you still thrills me
I love you so much that it kills me.
I have no complaints. I wanted a life without restraints
The very day we met.
We instantly grew together as a pair
The tinder times we've shared
I can never forget.
World showing us both signs
The feeling of your body
being close to mine.
It's like nothing that I've
Known at any other time
I felt what real love is
looking into your eyes
I want to immortalize
all in your view.

I see something magical
in all the things you do
The dearest thoughts I have
are the memories of you.

#Proud Father #Author #Poet #Health&FitnessAdvocate
#StoryTeller #Healing-Writer #Inspirational Speaker #Certified
Anti-HumanTraffickingAdvocate
Allpoetry.com/Matthew_Descovia

[Ganesh Eashwar]

Requiem!

Last Spring and Summer
My heart
Forgot to beat.
It sang.

Then came Autumn
You shed me.
Like the trees
Their leaves.

Came Christmas
And the New Year.
Both had Eves
But not I.

Spring's back again.
At last!
And my heart
Still sings.

Only Requiems!

———————————

Ganesh Eashwar. Indian Gypsy. Advertising. Organic Foods. Outspoken. Critical. But not Cynical. Yet! Hopes to move closer to the Himalayas, where he & his wife plan to spend the sunset of their lives. Allpoetry.com/Ganesh_Eashwar

[Philippe R Hebert]

Christmas of 1958

Remembering
Christmas of 1958
A visiting priest
Came to the house

I clearly remember
He began to sing acapella
O Holy night, in French
Minuit Cretin

He had come from a monastery
In Quebec
His treatment for tuberculosis
Left him pale and hair pure white

His voice so strong and pure
I began to cry
Like a baby
Unable to contain my emotions

───────────────

Philippe R. Hebert has written over 50 technical articles that have been published in various technical magazines. He is final negotiations with a publicist for his poetry book "Homage, An Anthology". Allpoetry.com/PRHebert

[Bobbie Breden]
Lost in the Fire ~~ Free Verse

Inspired by "Song of the Terrible" by Hilda Morley

On this chill autumn night, we rest before the fire
The day spent raking leaves,
And I, absently searching
For that one gloriously impeccable
And consummate emblem of Mabon

It ran to me on a breath of wind, rolling to my feet
Twin lobed, deeply veined, unblemished
Exquisitely symmetrical, perfect
Scarlet as wine, as intensely red
As cruor that forms over a pin prick

Now, I watch the fire, the undulating flames,
And you as you lay sleeping, your head in my lap,
The splendid leaf between your fingers,
The cozy fire that blazes in our hearth,
The sublime love that burns brightly within me

This love, wonderful and terrible, that warms me,
With your tender voice that sparks my heart,
Your smile that casts the light of a thousand suns
Your touch, a smoldering in my substance,
Melting me like wax

If I had a voice, I would sing to you a song of fire
Terrible fire, wherein I have reduced to ash
Images of past loves gone wrong,
Wonderful fire, resurrecting love and life
For without the spark of your love, I am but kindling

But for now, all is quiet
Save the cracking of the fire
And the sound of your breathing
And I am lost in the fire
And my love of you

_____

Retired Lady Leatherneck (US Marine), Renaissance woman, and a lover of life's mysteries. I'm interested in how others view the universe, and welcome opportunities to see it through their eyes. Allpoetry.com/Captain_B2

[Rachel Claire]

Dimentia

There's a story I've heard,
But it's distorted,
Slurred.
Mama, you don't make sense
Your words are blurred
Your tongue loses its footing
My stomach curdles.
I can see you struggle
through the cerebral hurdle.

Mama, do you hear me?
I know your mouth is fertile
With pain and pain and pain.
There's a litany in grief
In mourning your brain.
Dementia sweeps the contents of your head
Until your synapses are dead.
In cognizant dissonance
Your teeth chatter in innocence
a code of things unsaid. Mama, I
slither the scalpel over your crown and
weep, the future is stark;
Your skull is dark.

Rachel writes to process, relate and feel. When she's not inhabiting her head, she lives in Washington D.C. where she's learning to share more with less. Allpoetry.com/Rachelclaire

[Robert Buck]

time peace

(is dis de buff bot?)
.. -. / - .... / -.... --. ... -. -. ... -. --.
ⓣⓗⓔ ⓜⓔⓛⓞⓓⓡⓐⓜⓐ ⓜⓤⓢⓣ ⓟⓡⓞⓒⓔⓔⓓ
following are precious ◯🅟🅔🅐🅡🅛🅢◯
10-8 in service
Cast on
$X^0=1.00$
🕐
startling r**ef**∠ⓔχ reactions send
🅜🅔🅢🅢🅔🅝🅖🅔🅡🅢
for our protection
(last ditch, save
your day, gofers, express
the fairest freshest freakiest fervency)
1 of the strait signalers - up by 7
& a second's - minus five
they are however
all con-si-de-
red...≅
(& are re-
♻cycled de-
pending on the
karmic nature and
humanistic condition
of each improvised and
impoverishing identification)

2.

🕒

INSTINCT

...therewithal...

zoo-cred

(latterly

adulterated)

(animalistically

streeeet savvvvy)

r their snappy overall(s)

declared in each beginning

and they still mean it by the end

(symbolizing a singular spirit - that which -

follows the rabid frenzy in the host's absence)

when we are indeed initially and instantane-

ously (and) frequently missing persons

in the face of life's often sudden

traumatic crises, but we lose

our~~selves~~ much more e-

ven still, whilst watch-

fulness waxes-

wee willllll

wane

3.

🕒

(M0rtaLs 山廾0

aŘe naturally

ANTI-

PO-

DAL)

...fancy...
rituals
k👀kies n
🍪🍪🍪🍪
crème de la crème
🎩🎩🎩🎩🎩
apex apogees
(the best of the best)
saluting celebrations
regardless of outcomes
(pointless occurrences) the
intentionalities are commanding
✝ and let's hear it for **pilgrimages!**
the roundtrips we all take
↻ called 🔄 life ↻

4.
🕐
🅘🅝-
🆆🅴🅰🆅🅴
(basically complex)
multidimensionality
appropriately scheduled
O̶N̶ many A̶N̶O̶T̶H̶E̶R̶ P̶L̶A̶N̶E̶s
- what - jibes - where - with - when -
c o - m e m e s h m e n t*
===sss ttt sacred en masse
knitting 🧵 of holy
concepts
with

a
compadre
(becoming balanced)
↑ a profane pronouncement ↑
♋ ■ ♎ ♋ • ♦ ☐ ♦ ♋ ♦ ♐ ♦ ♎ ♑ ♏ ♎
*note novel nomenclature
⇧⇧⇧northward⇧⇧⇧
5.
🕐
DIVINE DESIGN
...genius...(evolution) 〖all t o -
g e t h e r /now\ i n t a n d e m〗
triggered extemporaneouslylylyly
often caught scrambling**
(𝔗𝔞𝔯𝔨𝔢𝔫𝔱𝔬𝔫'𝔰 𝔱𝔯𝔞𝔫𝔰𝔣𝔬𝔯𝔪)
f$_{o^r}$ $_{the}$ ^{r}i^g$_{ht}$ w$_a$y $_{to}$ play
(observe unemotionally
yr survival sense af the fact)
6.
🕐
CONSULT CON-
NOISSEURS
...housekeeping...
(process ^{101})
addedly assayed

unloosing loops
& slo-mo-ing b⃗ l⃗ u⃗ r⃗ s⃗
∽TRAIGHTEN∽ ∽UB∽TANTIATION
(a liaison with a dummy^ or a mannikin or a coat tree

191

is highly recommended or possibly a professional or an ancestor)

^: one who has not read 'Psychology For Dummies'

7.

🕑

CATCHING TOO-TOOS
TO THE TWOTH

...........the rub

(^{process} 22^2)

turninginging

stickyyyy pages

"**"cruelly steals"**"

costly sequential cycles

risking the wrong most recent

eventuality (bothered and bewildered)

(to dwell foretells a compelling

stagnation and transmogri-

fies the native path)

8.

🕑

...mercy...

SENILITY
SUSPENDERS

ʊPShƋƖ b$_{loo}$d c$_{lot}$ ^{hotspots}

eithera ripe-fail ora green-truth

ׅ('(·could be an old oath ora raw goof

the grace of God is a sporadic recourse

deciding≇¿momentarily each and every fate

(10-34 trouble at this station, help needed 👋)

(wave delay ΔΔΔΔΔ - ≈ = ≈ - ΔΔΔΔΔ faulty relay)

yet, the operation is interrupted by short erratic freezes

once our brains begin to fragment, tangle and be clogged,
namely and narrowly a new day paradisaically gushes futurology
so quicken your pace and strengthen your comprehension to fathom
the deeps (stay the symptoms of a and d, ∧|∨, whatever else may
have compromised your Chi(chē)~read, research and write on
***All Poetry*)**
ẑn̂t̂hlîĵk̂rϕr̂ϑϕẑϕz©® ^{SM}%‰%$_u$¹⁄₈^{TEL} ℗ ‰№ª⁄$_c$%⁄₈⊘☻✈

9.

🕓

(unless, unfortunately, u happen 2b allergic to
your own dope...then.......no one is safe)

10.

🕓

▓▓▶—=YER OUT!=—◀▓▓

♦ ♒ ♏ ♏ ■ Ω

温浦ひ

🐛🐌

Bind off

...

--

oops

epilog

11.

🕓

🄷🄰🅃-

🄲🄷🄸🄽🄶

🄱🄾🄾-🄺🄾🄾🅂 🄾🄵

🄱 🄾 🄾 - 🄱 🄾 🄾 🅂

§m̲u̲t̲a̲t̲i̲o̲n̲s̲

chancing childing changers

create⁵ curious creatures

et too spawn improves

opti-■■■■■-mollies

& octa-mummies

grow ragtags

and bobtails

full of behooves

AaIAIaXₐIXIx☐☐☐☐☐

little, big, blended and closed

♥n♥o♥s♥y♥ ♥a♥n♥d♥ ♥o♥i♥l♥y♥

■ yas ■ yes ■ yis ■ yos ■ yus ■

tombstone, halmos, end-of-proof

quod erat demonstrandum

typographic *end s ymbol*

(10-100 gotta go no.1)

⚠ ※ 🈲 ✘ 📢 ! ▷ ⚡

yield your yarramans

kick your heels and

pull in your horns

lol and behold

there is time

for II more

genuine

gems

PS

12.

🕛

🅞🅟🅣🅘🅜🅘🅢🅣🅘🅒

OBSERVATION
* * * all manifestations are prefaced positively * * *
we are presently and forever always as good as we can be
variable attributes exist dependently and follow exclusive rules
acceptance therefore is on an *either all or none* rationalization
sc; we cannot be peaceful without contemporary conflict
the being of binary (☿) turns on ternary '?:' >> ooo
a̅l̅l̅ s̅u̅r̅v̅e̅y̅e̅d̅ s̅t̅a̅t̅e̅s̅, s̅y̅s̅t̅e̅m̅s̅ & s̅e̅x̅e̅s̅ a̅r̅e̅ v̅a̅l̅i̅d̅

celestial vincula: heavenly bonds
♫entanglement entails - spooky tangos♫
13.

NO 'CLOCK, NO CONTROL
AND NO CHARACTERIZATION
❄ individuals are forbidden from inherent individuations
nurture of nature tones the personality sets with karmic codes
howbeit the sequels are preponderantly untested
thus, the accounts of amazing adaptability,
mt a modest modification, bi-ˈhā-vyə-
rə-lē speaking (that is) and then
calmly consider the corollary
(*We* d o *the* d u t y *of*
experimental robots)
10-20ogottagono2
cut the yarn
ᴛʜᴇ ɛη∂
10-7
out
of
s
e

195

r
v
i
c
e

∞∞

"Some
cause happiness
whe *r* ever they go; others
whe *n* ever they go" Oscar Wilde.
1 ϴ- 4 Ⓖ*ỖÔ*Đ B U***Dd***𝕀e𝐬
10-99 mission accom-
plished, all units
secure
✓✓✓
ETX
###

I am aka bobbing and a Tulsa lifer (so far). I have enjoyed versing and conversing for over ten years at AllPoetry. This poem is over the top for me and was more fun than an octogenarian should have. Allpoetry.com/bobbing

[S. Libellule]
Memory

"Memory is a warm coat" ~ Joy Harjo

Thick and threadbare
it buttons in the front
keeping out winds of doubt
handstitched with a tender care
full of a loving warmth
drapes over each shoulder

protects us when we are older

Originally from New England, Libellule currently lives outside of Birmingham, Alabama. Poetic influences include Mary Oliver, Billy Collins and ee cummings.   Allpoetry.com/Little_Dragonfly

[William Connelly, PhD]
The Fledgling Finally Flies

Another day has slipped away,
the sun has come and gone.
And in the night I hope I might
enjoy a new day's dawn.

The month of May has slipped away,
the moon has come and gone.
Though having fun in the summer sun
for another spring long.

Yet robins sing and children dream
as the sun begins to rise.
One life ends while another begins
and the fledgling finally flies.

One autumn day they flew away,
no more robins sing.
Now songless trees lose their leaves
'till robins return in spring?

It's been a year since we last past here
as Earth orbits the sun.
'Twas year with cheers and occasional tears
but finally spring has come.

Now robins sing and plants grow green
and humming birds grace the sky.
Most winter kill will surely heal
and fledglings soon will fly.

Bill is a geologist who enjoys various forms of writing. Many of his geological adventures are summarized in his book 'Tales of a Little Known Geologist' (Amazon). Allpoetry.com/Connelly

[Martha Enedina Gaytan]

My Daughter

Did you ever come across "that" girl that just made your neurotypical childs T-ball team lose? That was my daughter. "That" girl that her mother had to run to each base as she fought her mother to run because of her anxiety? That was my daughter. But, at the end of the season it was the same girl that carried her pride, dignity and ribbon acceptance in her smile!

When that teenager that just walked by throws a screaming tantrum in the middle of the store and all eyes are on her.
All shoppers eyes immediately turn, immediately whisper, immediately judge the parenting skills and the lack of attention she must be getting at home.
As her parents walk with their head up with their screaming teenager and not giving into her irrational need to purchase every barbie on that shelf.
I refuse to look at the strangers, I refuse to give into my uncomfortable situation, I refuse to give an apology because my child just had a behavior that her 5 year old mind could not control.

Parents anticipate a diagnosis, most cry and breakdown when they hear those words but, in reality those are the words that set them free.
After the diagnosis, you learn to begin the journey on how to help your little human to maneuver life, or your little human helps you to maneuver life their way.

Neurotypical children don't come with an instructional manual but, they have milestones guidelines.
Milestone? Milestone? We don't set the milestones..
the milestones are the biggest pride life changing moments in our lives.
My mindset is that small victories like my new found core values are without a finish line.

A special needs child will push your limits to the max...
Patience was not in my vocabulary. My boys can attest to that....
She taught me patience...
I should rephrase that... not taught me... she gave me a violent push into patience with a new perspective....
One step at a time, one moment at a time.

We try to teach our children about life, but our children teach us what life is all about.
Start every day as a fresh day, to be taught a new way, to slow down, to see life itself
outside the box.
Every teacher, advocate, peer, councilor, doctor and specialist deserve to be listed individually not to mention her brothers and father... because they have not just performed their job but have changed my daughters life, her entire families life. Their input and presence in her life have molded her into who she is today.... she has hit her own milestones with them on her side.
My teenager might not recite a poem by heart, might not be a pro runner but she carries her pride and dignity better than anyone I know and for that she will always be my princess and my special girl.

My daughter has taught me more than I have taught her ... in this lifetime.

_____

Martha Enedina Gaytan - I currently live in Bakersfield, CA. Poetry is new in my life and I would like to share with other special needs parents that they are not alone. Allpoetry.com/Martha_Enedina_Gaytan

[Lisa F. Raines]
Will you give love and stay?

Underlying power and
Movement of the waters
Nature is the course
Guiding our universe

Waves, crashing
Tumbling together
Entangled strings of
Men of war

Memories of near and far
And of who we are
Beholding our nature
What will be your future?

Do we give back
Or take a blessing
And run away
Will you give love and stay?

———————

AlisRamie is from North Carolina, USA.
Interests include: philosophy, history, international relations, politics, poetry, art, design, jazz, funk, and some good old soul.
Allpoetry.com/AlisRamie

[Rhiannon Bishop]

Ghost on a cliff

I sit on the bench where we always would,
On the rocky cliff, overlooking the Pacific Ocean
The crashing waves would sway us to sleep
As we look up, seeing a flock of geese flying home
Oh, how we envied those birds, free to fly wherever
Their wings, able to deliver them to a blissful heaven
Yet just like a blue sky, nothing perfect could last forever
On the night of our final farewell, the golden sunlight
Sheltering us in it's warmth, to hide the truth
Sounds of roaring thunder in the distance clang like cymbals
We look up as the birdcalls fill our empty ears
The geese overhead, soaring to the sun
One day hoping to be able to reach such nirvana
Oh, how you envied those birds, free to fly wherever
You yearned to go to the sun with them, so you did
But today, I sit here alone, I long to feel you here
Pining for a return that would never occur
The white seafoam against the rocks
It looks different now than when we first met here
Of course, the Earth eroding our love away
Like we were a simple page in a novel
I still feel you here, our love lost with a lonesome leap
You left me here alone, a single, lost ghost atop this now bleak and grey cliff,
overlooking of what was now a simple body of water

I look up to see the geese flying home
Oh, how I envy those birds, free to fly wherever,
They can fly home, but yet,
Why can't I?

———————————

Rhiannon Bishop, born and raised in rural Pennsylvania

I have always wanted to write poems, inspired by my great grandfather who also would enjoy writing, able to escape the world as we know it Allpoetry.com/Rhiannon_Bishop

[Shanayah P. Tyrna-Denman]
Have you ever heard of the crying river fairy?

Have you ever heard of the crying river fairy?
They say her tears fall down her rosy cheeks like crystals. Turning her head and staring right through your soul, but the feeling that erupts through your core is one that is heavenly and enchanted by her beauty. One never knows why she cries, but her movements that sway so easily through the soft wind, makes you want to keep looking. Those wings that sparkle under the moonlight and the hair that glisten and shine. You cannot help but ask yourself *why would anyone make such a goddess cry such tears.?*Suddenly with a halt she stopped her beautiful dance, a smile gently appears upon those soft pinkish lips, as she herself got closer. With a gentle voice, the fairy says, *the one you should call a fairy, a goddess is yourself, you are in pain, I am you, you are me.*Gently brushing my cheek with her hand, slowly walking away and vanishing in thin air.

Shanayah, also known as Shay, is from Queensland, Australia.

I like writing poetry and coming up with storylines in this brain of mine. It is a way of calming my mind with these flooding thoughts. Allpoetry.com/Shay_Paige

[Jeremy Geld]
Hatred

Why not?
Give me a reason
Not the reason you were handed down
I want yours

Through the abyss
I floated in the cold
And floated
And floated

A darkness setting in
A numbness
A blindness

A blindness so strong
There was nothing left.

Jeremy is from Seattle, WA. He likes rainy days and bright autumn oranges. He forgot he liked poetry. But now he has remembered. Allpoetry.com/Kartoffel

Made in United States
Orlando, FL
16 January 2023